To Judge Rosenblatt

In the hope that mediation of family disputes helps to reduce the burden on the court system.

warm regards

Bob G⎯

Oct 12, 88

FIGHTING FAIR

FIGHTING FAIR

*Family Mediation
Will Work for You*

Robert Coulson

THE FREE PRESS
A Division of Macmillan, Inc.
NEW YORK

Collier Macmillan Publishers
LONDON

The Free Press
A Division of Macmillan, Inc.
866 Third Avenue, New York, N.Y. 10022

Collier Macmillan Canada, Inc.

Printed in the United States of America

printing number

1   2   3   4   5   6   7   8   9   10

Library of Congress Cataloging in Publication Data

Coulson, Robert.
  Fighting fair.

  Bibliography: p.
  Includes index.
  1. Family life education.   2. Marriage counseling.
3. Divorce mediation.   4. Counseling—Vocational
guidance.   I. Title.
HQ10.C67   1983   362.8′286   82-25117
ISBN 0-02-906420-1

Contents

Acknowledgments

IN PREPARING THIS BOOK, I received help and encouragement from many practicing mediators and family lawyers. Some are quoted in the text. Others are listed in the bibliography. In addition, I was greatly assisted by Paula Fitz, a summer intern from Cornell University, who collected a mass of information. I also want to express my thanks to Dorothy Hans and many other friends at the American Arbitration Association who helped with this work, particularly to Tom Colosi, Bob Meade, and Midge and Josh Stulberg, who have shown a sustained interest in family mediation, and to Phil Thompson, who initially encouraged me to write this book.

I am much in debt to many people who have been trying to bring mediation forward as a responsible, useful system for resolving family disputes. H. Jay Folberg, Sheila Kessler, Mark Lohman, Ann Milne, Jessica Pearson, Professor Frank E. A. Sander, Linda Singer, and Janet Spencer deserve particular thanks. Finally, in writing about divorce mediation, it is appropriate to give credit to the contributions of the late O. J. Coogler, a troubled but creative pioneer in this field.

Introduction

PEOPLE ARE SAYING that the old-style American family is changing rapidly, popping like corn on a hot plate. The two-parent home has become an endangered habitat. What is your opinion? Think now. How is your own family holding up?

More people are living alone. Mothers and fathers alike are bringing up one or more children with no spouse in the home. People are living together in unrelated groups. When kids grow up, they leave home. Older people get shunted off into geriatric enclaves. What still remains of the old-fashioned American family?

During the 1960s and seventies, government began to poke its nose into family affairs, which was easy to do because the federal government was willing to provide subsidies or professional help. Federal and state laws gave family courts and welfare departments the authority to intervene, placing children in foster care, mandating social services, and providing fiscal support in unprecedented amounts. Some families lost interest in running their own affairs. They gave up. But many families rejected government intervention. They demanded the right to manage their own lives.

This book is about family mediation, a relatively new way to help family members deal with their problems. Mediation encourages people to resolve their own disagreements. It represents a new service, perhaps a new profession, assisting family members to fight fair, to settle disputes in a sensible way. Helping people can be satisfying. Too many of us spend our time working, sleeping, watching television, driving around wondering what to do. Many Americans have been indulgent, enjoying greedy lives, accumulating things but losing something in the process. There must be more to life than that.

Family mediation provides a way to serve other people. This book tells how mediation can settle various kinds of family disputes and explains how the reader can become a mediator. Moreover, mediation can be a technique for self-help. If you are troubled by family disputes of your own, mediation may provide a solution. By learning to think like a mediator, you can build constructive ideas into your own behavior.

When I first gave a lecture on divorce mediation at the annual convention of the Family Law Section of the American Bar Association in 1974, in Atlanta, Georgia, several lawyers scoffed at the suggestion. They said it would never work. The idea did seem radical at that time. Now the wind has shifted. Many attorneys refer their own clients to divorce mediators. Some have learned to mediate themselves. There is no shortage of work. More than a million divorces are granted each year in the United States. According to the census, the number of families headed by divorced women has tripled in the past ten years. There are more than three million single-parent households. One out of every five children lives with a single parent, usually the mother. Divorce mediation has become acceptable. In some states, family courts even require couples to see a conciliator before a divorce will be granted. Hundreds of private divorce mediators have hung out their shingles. Wonderful! Anything to keep family problems out of court. Anything to encourage families to resolve their own problems.

A breakup of a marriage is an everyday event. Divorce mediation can make the process less painful. Mediation can work with other kinds of family disputes. Squabbles over who should support an elderly parent. Disputes about a contested will. When your son obtains a driver's license, how often should he have use of the family car? How will that question be decided? When your teenage daughter wants an abortion, who will pay the doctor's bill? You or her boyfriend? If you wait for a court to decide, you may end up sending your grandchild through college. Other examples come easily to mind. Contests over an adopted child. Fights to control a family business. Problems with delinquent adolescents. Such matters often end in court. It would be better for the family to resolve them privately.

Unrelated people encounter problems as well. When tenants share an apartment, how do they decide their quarrels? Who gets to keep the apartment when roommates split up? How does a homosexual collect a debt from a lover? How should a fiancée break off an engagement at the last minute? How about the engagement ring?

This book encourages readers to think like mediators. It may not be easy to act as a mediator. Parties are not always willing to trust a stranger with their problems. But if you do succeed, you will feel pretty good about yourself. Hundreds of social workers, family therapists, and attorneys already serve as mediators. Thousands more will soon enter the field. For some, mediation provides a new outlet for their professional skills. For others, it offers new insights about themselves and the people close to them.

Even if you don't expect to serve as a mediator, the process should interest you. In resolving your own problems, mediation can be helpful. In *America Without Vio-*

lence (1982), Professor Michael N. Nagler, of the Berkeley Peace Studies Project, makes that point:

> The way to use mediation with potentially unlimited effectiveness. . . . *Be your own mediator.* Personal style is the beginning, a style in which the mediator's detachment is, so to speak, internalized. And the way to get upstream with this technique is by striving to use it constantly, not waiting until conflict and violence have erupted. A life style informed by this technique means facing others with an entirely different attitude than that encouraged by modern conditions and modern conditioning, an especially difficult task when we feel the configuration of conflict closing in.

As Nagler explains, "to listen unfailingly to an opponent's point of view, indeed even to recognize that he or she has a point of view, is a powerful mechanism for resolution." It is not only fair to try to understand your opponent's point of view, it is sensible. By looking at the case in a fair-minded way, you will understand it better.

No matter how complicated the issues may be, mediation will work. A mediator need not be the world's greatest expert on every aspect of the controversy to be settled. This is as true in family disputes as in international negotiations or collective bargaining of a labor conflict. By concentrating upon the mediation process, by encouraging the parties to negotiate their own settlement, a mediator can contribute to the solution. Mediation does not force an outside judgment upon the parties. The mediator allows the parties themselves to weave their own values and desires into an acceptable settlement, helping them to fight fair.

1

Mediating Family Disputes

MEDIATION ENCOURAGES FAMILIES to fight fair. It enables them to control their own disputes. It also provides a powerful learning experience. With the help of a mediator, they learn who they are and what they truly want.

Mediation is not for everyone. Some people require therapeutic help. They may be incapable of dealing with adversarial stress. In other situations, a court order may be necessary to force an individual to negotiate in good faith. If someone is unwilling to bargain, mediation can't proceed.

Family controversies come wrapped in a thick gauze of past relationships. The inner core of the problem may be impenetrable. A mediator can only try to demystify the issue, encouraging the participants to consider the possibility of a commonsense solution. Family mediation is not a panacea. It works for some parties, certainly not for all. It does provide an opportunity for people to settle their dispute equitably, reasonably and directly. That is what fighting fair is all about.

What is the alternative? If the parties can't work things out, they may have to go to court for a determination. In that event, they must hire lawyers and follow the traditional adversary process. In an article in *California Living,* M. J. Perry (1980) describes the typical result for a divorcing couple:

> Divorce is never easy. Nearly all divorced spouses feel anger, hurt and guilt to varying degrees. When you add two adversary lawyers hovering and trained to argue and conquer, you often end up with hostility and bitterness and sometimes expensive litigation. The "let your lawyer fight it out with my lawyer" approach often leads to more controversy than intended.

When family disputes have to be decided in court or when they are negotiated by lawyers under the threat of litigation, the family members may find themselves involved in a battle that brings out the most spiteful and destructive aspects of their character. Mediation offers an alternative. A trained mediator can help parties regain control of their own dispute. The negotiation process makes it possible for them to sit down together in an effort to understand what must be done about their future, to concentrate upon resolving their problems, and to capture whatever remains of their mutual trust. This book describes the problem-solving potential that permeates mediation and the negotiating process.

But let's start at the beginning. Let's think about the family. Many people are worried about its future. Can it be saved?

Has the family become obsolete?

The American family is under heavy stress. Families are smaller: for seventeen consecutive years, the size of the average household has declined, to 2.72 persons at present. Falling birth rates, increased numbers of working mothers, liberal sexual mores, nomadic lifestyles, and an expanding welfare state have threatened the integrity of the family. Young people are questioning the need to get married. Many couples are breaking up. Foster care is rampant.

According to the Census Bureau, 18.9 million Americans were living alone in 1981. Many were elderly, but 22 percent of the women between twenty-five and twenty-nine had never been married. In the same year, there were 10.8 million divorced people, not including those who had remarried. As a result, a vast number of children were living in single-parent homes: 12.6 million Americans under the age of eighteen, or more than 20 percent of this age group, lived with only one parent in 1981. Looking at those kinds of statistics creates some doubt about the future of the family.

Do not despair. The family has shown a remarkable ability to meet new challenges. It is still our primary socializing institution. But it is changing. New lifestyles have evolved: single people living alone, married couples without children, unmarried couples, and groups, some of whose members may be children. These may not be traditional families, but they are families nonetheless. They are people living together, sharing the obligations and advantages of family life.

Many people still live in traditional families, supported by a father, serviced by a mother, with two or more children. Others are following a different pattern. There is diversity. Americans are free to select their own lifestyle. In diversity, there may be strength.

Look at the bright side. Increasing numbers of women are wage earners, exerting control over their own destinies. They are able to provide for themselves. As they find work, they acquire more independence within their households than ever before.

Our population is maturing. As these self-sufficient people settle into chosen lifestyles, they yearn for familylike stability. Groups of adults who pool their resources on a voluntary basis are not held together by the same pressures that encourage nuclear families to remain intact. Such households are sustained by ties of friendship or by practical needs. As we shall see, in such circumstances, disputes may be less easy to settle than disagreements in the traditional family.

The household is our primary unit of social organization for two very good reasons. It is efficient and we Americans are practical people. Thus, we continue to believe in family life, whatever guise it takes. Communal living provides a secure base for people's daily lives. These notions go far toward guaranteeing the survival of the family.

Is it O.K. for families to fight?

Being able to disagree is healthy. A conflict-free relationship is undesirable, if not unattainable. Indeed, quarrels are stimulating. Even more important, they encourage the growth and change that leads to individual development. Families should fight but should do so in a positive way. As you read on, you will learn how to negotiate effectively and how to avoid squabbling in a way that is only destructive and spiteful.

Successful conflict management requires intellectual honesty. Members of a family must feel free to express themselves. A healthy relationship involves trust and sharing. Arguments provide an opportunity for family members to enjoy the give-and-take of living together. This can be particularly important for adolescent children who need an opportunity to test their adversary skills against an adult. For them, negotiating will provide a key to the adult world.

This is not to say that every disagreement must be resolved. With adolescents, parents can expect flurries of selfish behavior and blizzards of confrontation. It would be impossible to resolve all such disputes. They have to be absorbed as necessary episodes on the way to maturity.

Is someone usually to blame in family fights?

It is never easy to fix blame. The person who seems to have caused the problem may have been provoked. Someone else may have made a crisis inevitable, pushing the situation beyond the point of reconciliation. Why did the provocation take place? Was it intentional? Did either party understand what was happening?

A mediator is not a judge. Parties have to make their own settlement. The mediator can only help them to resolve their dispute by redirecting their efforts away from trying to determine who was to blame. The parties must learn to stop blaming each other and concentrate upon solving their problems. Parties must deal with their future.

When a dispute arises in your own family, don't start out by attempting to assign blame. In most cases, that is a waste of time. Life is not a game of cops and robbers. Think like a mediator. Forget the past. Look toward the future. Stop playing the "blame game."

What is mediation?

Mediation is a process by which an impartial third person (sometimes more than one person) helps parties to resolve disputes through mutual concessions and face-to-face bargaining. A divorce mediator works with a couple on how they will live apart after their separation. Family mediators help work out settlements in other kinds of interpersonal disputes.

The mediator does not force parties to settle their dispute but tries to convince them that they and their family will benefit from reaching an agreement. The mediator helps the parties understand what is happening to them and warns them how difficult their life will become if they are unable to agree. The mediator encourages the parties to negotiate in good faith and to enter into arrangements that will be enforceable in future years.

Do people have to use a mediator?

Of course not. A mediator operates at the pleasure of the parties. Any of the parties can dismiss the mediator at any time. Under the Family Mediation Rules of the American Arbitration Association, mediation is entirely voluntary.

The parties should always be free to break off the mediation. The dispute belongs to them. For that reason, mediation is the least threatening of all settlement processes. If it works, fine. If it does not work, the parties can try something else. They can give up. They can consult another mediator. They can attempt to settle their dispute without a mediator. They can go to court.

At the same time, a mediator does not have to continue working for the parties and may decide that they are wasting their time because they are not serious about wanting to settle their dispute.

Why do parties use a mediator?

Most family disagreements are resolved without mediation. Parties work out the problem by themselves, but sometimes parties need help. This is particularly likely in a crisis: a threatened divorce, serious delinquency on the part of a child, a fight for control of a family business, or some other situation that requires substantial concessions within the family. Then an experienced mediator can be helpful.

The parties must be willing to negotiate. If they won't talk to each other about their problem, mediation can't help. Most people believe that family relationships are important. This prompts them to make concessions in order to resolve arguments. Only in unusual circumstances are people willing to abandon their entire family.

This desire for family continuity is not so obvious when a husband and wife are negotiating a separation. Each individual may be bitter and anxious to fight. Even then, most couples realize that they will have to accept certain mutual obligations and restraints. Support payments must be paid on schedule. Visitation rights must be honored. And other commitments have to be met that will benefit various members of the family.

What happens in a typical mediation?

Karen Irvin of the Minnesota Mediation & Counseling Center sent me a description of a typical divorce mediation case.

Bob and Cathy were referred by a friend. Wanting to minimize the cost of their divorce, they thought that they would try mediation before retaining legal counsel. They had been married for six years. This was Bob's first marriage, the second for Cathy. Cathy's daughter from her first marriage lived with them. They had no children from their own marriage. Both were employed. Bob's salary was $37,500. Cathy's was $21,000. When they came to the center, they were still living in the same house and sharing expenses. They had been talking to a marriage counselor for eighteen months. They didn't want to hurt each other. The unresolved issues between them seemed to focus on the distribution of their assets and liabilities. Child custody and support and alimony were not involved. At the outset, Bob and Cathy expressed a willingness to be fair.

The center decided to use two mediators, one male and one female, because each party preferred someone of the same sex. Although the primary issues were financial, emotional elements were also likely to arise. Co-mediators could bring different areas of expertise to these issues.

The first mediation session ran two hours. The items to be negotiated were identified. Each party began to blame the other for what had happened during the marriage. They seemed preoccupied with expressing their feelings. The mediators encouraged them to do so. Little else was accomplished.

In an attempt to make progress, the mediators began

the next session by requesting each party to concentrate on the items in dispute. Bob and Cathy were able to reach agreement fairly quickly on several issues. Both were able to talk about their concerns for the future. This process proved beneficial. They also agreed to develop proposals for resolving the remaining issues, presenting them at the next session.

Both parties were less agreeable at the start of the third session. They had attempted to divide their personal property but had argued. The mediators needed to remind Bob and Cathy to work together rather than fight. The mediators listed all of the property on a display board and asked Bob and Cathy to identify the items not in dispute. These were removed from the list. Cathy was then asked to make a proposal relative to one item on the list. Bob was asked his opinion about Cathy's proposal. He expressed his approval, conditional on his getting something else on the list. This process went on until only one or two very small items remained on the list. Then, Bob and Cathy became stubborn. The remaining items symbolized the end of their relationship, and parties sometimes stall at this point. Finally, a settlement of the assets was concluded. Because the assets included real property, the parties were encouraged to consult a lawyer about the tax impact of the proposed distribution.

The fourth mediation session was relatively uneventful. The parties were comfortable with the process and discussed the division of their debts in a straightforward manner. When a final understanding was reached, the mediators reviewed the entire agreement.

Cathy and Bob wanted the mediators to explain the settlement to Cathy's daughter, Pam. The fifth session began by allowing Pam to ask questions. Then the mediators gave Cathy and Bob copies of their completed agreement. They were again encouraged to seek legal advice. In any case, a lawyer would handle the formal divorce.

The mediation required a total of nine hours over a period of seven weeks. The legal work took four weeks.

Mediation expenses were $525. Attorney fees totaled $350. In addition to achieving a fair settlement, Bob and Cathy maintained their friendship. They continued to entertain friends together after their divorce. Both of them expressed appreciation for the mediation process.

This case describes a successful divorce mediation. The parties were willing to negotiate. The mediators helped to facilitate a settlement. The outcome was satisfactory to the parties.

Parties turn to a mediator because they have decided that without such assistance, they may be unable to resolve their dispute. A friend or an adviser may have told them that they need professional help. Merely by going to a mediator, the parties already have expressed some willingness to compromise. The mediator must then convince them of the benefits of the process. Many people are not sure what mediation is supposed to do. The mediator should answer their questions, persuading the clients that the process is likely to result in a settlement. One of the parties to a dispute may be reluctant to go forward. A wife may hesitate to confront her husband. A child may be afraid to make demands on a parent. A parent may refuse to recognize a child's right to bargain. Thus, the mediator must persuade both parties to enter into negotiations.

An interesting mediation case appeared in the February 1982 *Colorado Lawyer*. The case, reported by Jessica Pearson of the Center for Policy Research in Denver, Colorado, involved a couple who had been married for nine years and who had two young children. The couple had been separated for over a year; the husband was living with another woman. The wife filed for divorce. Her husband demanded sole custody. Frustrated with the legal help they were receiving, the couple decided to try mediation.

The mediation took six sessions and resulted in an agreement. At first the parties expressed annoyance with each other, trading accusations. The mediator helped them explore areas of disagreement and provided practical ideas for solutions. By the second session, the couple was discussing custody. The mediator recommended that they read a book on joint custody and gave each of them a copy. By the third session, they were giving that idea serious thought. By then, they had learned to communicate more effectively and were beginning to understand each other's problems. They came to realize that they shared concern for their children. To help their kids, they would have to trust each other. By sessions four and five, the parties were working from a memorandum of agreement prepared by the mediator. One proposal provided for joint custody. They had been able to divide their household possessions and to work out an arrangement for child support and mortgage payments. During the sixth session, they were able to formalize their separation agreement.

Pearson concludes that mediation is less expensive, faster, and more satisfactory than court resolution in divorce cases. Moreover, couples who mediate are less likely to go to court later. Pearson thinks that attorneys should recommend divorce mediation to their clients.

Why can't families work out their own problems?

In a healthy family, negotiations occur constantly. People make demands and trade concessions every day. The process is automatic, so that the family may not even realize that it is happening. For such a family, there may be no need for an outside mediator. Some couples don't even need a mediator when they get a divorce.

On the other hand, splitting up family property or deciding upon the custody of children are difficult issues that many couples cannot resolve on their own. One divorce mediator put it this way: "Clients don't come to me because they enjoy my company. Usually they have looked into the expense of doing it with lawyers. They may have tried to do it themselves. When they decided that they needed help, someone sent them to me."

Does a mediator recommend a solution?

At the outset, a mediator does not know what the dispute is about. Only by working with the parties can a mediator begin to understand what needs to be done. Rule one: Don't shoot from the hip.

A couple may come to a mediator for a divorce. After the individuals talk about their problems, they may decide to stay married. Mendel H. Lieberman practices family mediation in California. He described such a case to me:

> Bill and Charlene first came to me with two teenage children. Don was sixteen. He seemed angry most of the time. Emily was a year younger. These children were Charlene's by a prior marriage. Bill also had children by a prior marriage; they lived with their mother. On weekends, Don and Emily went to their father. Bill's children came to Bill and Charlene. It wasn't working out. "You can't tell the players without a program," sneered Don. Ignoring him, Bill said, "Charlene and I would get along fine if it weren't for the kids." Charlene nodded.
>
> Don explained, "Bill has this big macho trip going. He wants to be the boss. Do it his way or get out of the house. But, then, he won't let us out of the house. I mean, it's like crazy in there." I asked Emily whether she saw it the same way. She shrugged: "I don't know." Bill's face turned red: "That's all we can get out of her: 'I don't know. I don't know.'" "Maybe she really doesn't know," Don suggested. Emily threw him a withering look. I turned to Bill: "What results would you expect from working with me?" "If you get Don to stop mouthing off———" Don interrupted sarcastically, "Yeah, get Don to change. How about you?" Charlene broke in, "You could both give a little, instead of always being at each other's throat." Then everyone talked at once. Everyone but Emily. A tear ran down her cheek. By this time I had some tentative impressions. The case had been presented as a dispute between Bill and Charlene, but the problem seemed more complex.

I like working with a family as a unit, but I made a date to see Bill and Charlene without the teenagers. Charlene opened the session by expressing her concern about Emily. Bill interrupted her frequently to "correct" details. Charlene finally exploded, "Don't keep interrupting me all the time." Turning to me, she said, "He always does that. With the kids too. It drives them crazy." "I notice that you speak for the kids," I said. "But how about you? How do *you* feel when he interrupts?" Charlene shrugged and looked toward Bill. "I think she's saying," Bill offered, "that she *feels* that I should not interrupt." Another miscommunication. I broke in. "That you shouldn't interrupt is not a feeling. It is a judgment or conclusion. Let's make a list of some feeling words."

We did. Bill and Charlene came up with words like angry, afraid, hopeless, depressed, lonely, uncomfortable, sick, frustrated. I added a few like proud, loving, hopeful, comfortable, confident. Charlene copied the words we had listed and put the list in her purse. She seemed excited. Bill expressed skepticism. Then I explained why feelings were important: "Each of us has very little power to make other people change but maximum power to change ourselves. Agreed?" They nodded. And so we looked at how Bill and Charlene could change. "I could be less rigid," Bill offered. "And I could stop letting him walk all over me," Charlene said. "Watch out about blaming," I warned. "It makes the other person defensive, and you wind up not getting what you want." "What am I supposed to do when he shames me in front of friends?" "You're exaggerating. I did that once. Maybe twice." Charlene dabbed at her eyes: "You always do it."

I broke in, "Instead of blaming, how would it be if you said, 'When you do that, I feel hurt?' Instead of 'You always interrupt me,' you could say 'When you interrupt me, I feel bad.' I like the way you are picking up on how to increase your effectiveness as individuals, but there may be room for you to increase your effectiveness as a couple. Try thinking of yourselves as an executive team. It may be that part of Don's acting out is a way of saying, 'Who is in charge here?' This does not mean that you must hide your differences from the kids. It does mean that you should make it clear to the kids that you are in charge *together* even when the two of you differ.''

This example shows how an experienced family mediator works. The mediator does not prejudge the family's problem. By listening carefully and by trying to resolve problems as they appear, the mediator helps the parties understand their options. For a mediator to make a settlement proposal early in the negotiations would be dangerous: It may be risky to even express an opinion at that time because one of the parties may decide that the mediator is not impartial. When the parties have indicated the direction in which they are moving, a mediator can recommend a formula based upon what seems to be acceptable. When a settlement is imminent, the mediator's intervention may close the gap.

Why trust a family mediator?

A family mediator must earn the parties' respect. An experienced mediator should have little difficulty in creating trust. The parties are novices. The mediator is likely to be an expert in family disputes.

Unless the parties believe that a mediator is effective, they may seek help elsewhere. At every session, the mediator must demonstrate an ability to assist the negotiations.

A family mediator has a precarious hold over the parties. Make one mistake and the game is lost. The mediator must walk a tightrope carrying the parties and their issues on both shoulders. One mediator put it this way: ''The only advantage I have going for me is that I have been around this track many times before. I can explain things that seem obvious, based on my experience. Unless a mediator is familiar with family problems, the parties may decide that they can do just as well on their own.''

Where can parties find a qualified and acceptable mediator?

Experienced family mediators are available. The American Arbitration Association keeps lists of family mediators at its twenty-five regional offices, but there are other sources as well. In many communities, independent family mediation agencies have been established. A 1982 *Dispute Resolution Program Directory,* published by the American Bar Association, listed 141 such programs. A similar *Directory of Mediation Services* was compiled by the Divorce Mediation Research Project of Denver in the same year. Jessica Pearson was the project director. Some pastoral counselors also offer family mediation, and family courts may provide conciliation services.

Before settling on a mediator, the parties should find out whether the mediator's approach is consistent with their own needs. At the initial interview, the parties should feel quite free to ask questions:

How does the mediator operate?

How much experience as a family mediator?

What training?

References?

What is the mediator's background?

How many sessions will be required?

How much will mediation cost?

Family mediation creates a close relationship: the parties should be certain that they have chosen the right person.

Is mediation expensive?

As I have noted, the parties should ask how much the mediator charges and how long the mediation is likely to take. These issues should be resolved at the first session. A rate should be fixed, by the hour or by the session, and it should be settled how the cost will be shared by the parties. Compared to court litigation, voluntary mediation is inexpensive.

Mediators may work without compensation. For example, a minister may offer such services free to members of the church. A friend of the family may volunteer to mediate a particular problem. Sometimes this service is subsidized by a family court. But in many situations, a mediator will charge a fee. The important point is that parties should know in advance what financial and time commitments mediation will involve. Also, they should be sure that they can terminate the process if they are not satisfied. Don't enter into an arrangement with a mediator without that assurance. It is your dispute. The mediator is working for you.

What can go wrong?

Even though parties can cancel the process at any time, there may be risk in turning to mediation. One danger is obvious. A party may be persuaded to agree to a bad settlement. A party may become emotional, eager to achieve a quick resolution. Unless one exercises restraint, one may be swept into an unwise concession. Parties shouldn't let themselves be pressured. Both parties should be sure that their settlement makes sense. The mediator should caution them on that score.

A quite different risk is that the mediator may block the parties' agreement by insisting upon unnecessary procedures. The parties should set their own pace. The negotiating process belongs to them. The mediator is there only to help.

Some family mediators are inexperienced. Parties should proceed cautiously until they have established confidence in their mediator's ability.

Cost is always a potential problem. Mediators usually bill on an hourly basis. A mediator may spend more time on your case than is justified. Parties should demand an explanation if charges seem high and should complain if they feel that the mediator has overcharged.

Most worrisome is the fear that a mediator will allow a strong party to exploit a weaker one whose interests may not be represented adequately in the negotiation. Will children be victimized by agreements that do not adequately protect their interests? There is no easy answer to this concern. Separation agreements must be submitted to court for confirmation, but other family settlements may not enjoy such protection. For example, an agreement between two brothers to share the cost of a nursing home for their parent, whether this is negotiated directly between the brothers or arranged with the help of a mediator, would not be subject to judicial review. Such an agreement might not even be reviewed by an attorney. If anything, the involvement of a mediator may add a measure of protection to all concerned. But the mediator does not guarantee that the agreement is fair. It is up to the individual parties to protect their own interests.

Some mediation centers restrict the parties' access to a personal attorney. For example, the Family Mediation Association will appoint a lawyer for a couple if the parties are unable to select one from a closed panel. The parties' personal lawyers would be excluded. This restriction causes concern. A party in a mediation should have the right to choose legal counsel freely.

Where should mediation sessions take place?

When parties meet with a mediator, they are likely to be under stress. A comfortable, informal setting can facilitate the mediation process.

Some mediators like to meet around a small table in a conference room. Others believe that any table hinders communication and prefer comfortable chairs in an open room. Some use a professional office because it provides an atmosphere of stability, indicating to clients that they are in responsible hands. The choice of ambience is a question of personal style.

Many mediators prefer that sessions take place in the office they use for their primary job as an attorney, therapist, or whatever. A mediator connected with an agency such as the American Arbitration Association can use its facilities. The mediator's image may be enhanced by the impartial reputation of such an organization. Moreover, clients can come to such a site without letting other people know that they are having family problems.

Every object in the room should be selected carefully. What message is being communicated to the parties? In a room dedicated to mediation, furnishings should be comforting. They should not express controversial values. A religious painting should not be placed directly in front of a wife who is complaining that her husband has abandoned the family's religion.

The mediator should be careful not to occupy a seat that appears to favor one party. The room should be surveyed in advance to assure that all parties will feel fairly placed.

Whether the meeting room is located in an office building or in a residence, it should exude security. The setting should be quiet, discreet, and convenient. Clean toilet facilities and adequate parking should be available.

Some family mediators provide coffee during sessions. Permitting the parties to smoke depends upon their preferences and upon the mediator's. One mediator serves alcoholic beverages after a settlement has been reached. I do not recommend this.

Sometimes the participants may be most comfortable mediating in their own home. Holding meetings there might emphasize that the mediator is a guest of the family. On the other hand, a residence is often full of distractions like telephones and doorbells. A too familiar setting also may detract from the process. Finally, as an outsider, the mediator may appear to have less authority than is desirable.

How many meetings will be necessary? When will they be held? How long will they take?

The first session will include both parties. At this meeting, a schedule should be developed. The parties and the mediator should estimate how many sessions are required. One purpose of mediation is to encourage parties to control their own lives. The mediator should let the parties participate in setting their own schedule. As much as possible, the mediator can be guided by the parties.

Some mediators like to meet frequently. Others prefer to schedule sessions several days apart. Again, this should be discussed with the parties. A decision will also have to be made about the length of the sessions.

Social workers and therapists who do mediation may like to fit parties into their professional schedule. Other mediators may be more flexible. "Totally a matter of style," one mediator explained. "I like to work with fifty-minute blocks. I see my other clients on that basis, so it is convenient for me to schedule mediation that way. For some clients, I make an exception. Usually, I see them in the evening or on weekends, with longer time allotments."

Family mediation sessions are often scheduled in the evening since one or more of the clients usually works during the day. Some mediators schedule sessions on weekends. Others like to keep regular office hours during the week.

Whether the sessions are limited to fifty minutes or are allowed to run on for an extended time depends upon the work habits of the mediator and the preferences of the parties. With experience, each mediator will develop a particular pattern. According to one successful California mediator, "It depends on how busy I am. When I began to build my practice, I really didn't care. I would spend an entire evening talking with one client. Now I am busier. I maintain an appointment book and try to keep sessions to the allotted time."

Does the mediator record what is said?

Most mediators take notes during the session. Some like to dictate a memorandum afterward. A few mediators use tape recorders. When doing so, the mediator should explain that the recording is for the mediator's confidential use. The tape will not be used for any other purpose.

At least one mediator uses videotape, particularly when preparing a party for a joint session. He plays the tape back to show how the presentation could have been strengthened. Video equipment can be invaluable in coaching a client in verbal skills. Also the technique demonstrates that the mediator is taking the case seriously.

While recordings can help a mediator remember exactly what was said and the tone in which certain information was conveyed, some people are inhibited by a recorder. Moreover, family mediators generally are reluctant to tape joint sessions. Parties should be encouraged to speak frankly. Often the intimate feelings that they are able to express provide the key to the ultimate settlement.

Can a mediator be forced to testify about what was said in the negotiations?

Mediation involves a confidential relationship. The American Arbitration Association's Family Mediation Rules provide that confidential information disclosed by the parties to a mediator may not be divulged. This rule is consistent with the present law.

The recommended retainer agreement contained in Appendix D includes a statement that the parties will not name the mediator as a party or a witness in any court proceeding or subpoena the mediator or any of the mediator's records.

What kinds of family problems can be mediated?

Many family disputes in addition to divorce negotiations are appropriate for mediation.

• *Disputes between unmarried adults.* According to the Census Bureau, there were 1.8 million unmarried couples in 1981. In such households, disputes may arise over who is responsible for paying rent. When space is in short supply, the parties may quarrel over who has the right to stay in the apartment.

Cases of this kind often come to the attention of mediators working with community programs established to handle neighborhood disputes. Nettie Good is a mediator with the Community Dispute Center (run by the American Arbitration Association) in Garden City, Long Island. One of her cases, involving an unmarried couple, was referred to the center by the district attorney of Nassau County. It involved a young Hispanic couple.

María was a Puerto Rican woman who had recently moved to Long Island. She shared an apartment with José, and they were lovers. José dated other women, but if María even looked at another man, he flew into a rage.

One night José came home drunk from his job. María tried to keep him out of their apartment. He broke open the door and threw the telephone at María's head. She went to the hospital with a fractured skull and covered with blood. After ten days, she went home to her family in San Juan.

When María returned to Long Island, she filed a criminal complaint against José. The case was referred to mediation. José admitted that he had been drinking beer. He complained that María had tried to stop him from coming into the apartment. Becoming angry, he had forced his way in. He admitted throwing the telephone at her. He just intended to scare her. José said that he loved María and had not meant to hurt her. Privately, María told the mediator that she was afraid to live with José. She liked to be with him but not when he was drunk.

María agreed to drop the charges against José if he would move out of the apartment. Each of them agreed to respect the other's privacy. José would pay María's hospital bill. When the lease ended on their apartment, José would return María's share of the security.

Mediator Good commented on the case: "These two young people were living in an unfamiliar community. Adjustments proved difficult for them. Neither had any family ties in Garden City. No one here cared how they behaved. Without supervision, they created an unfortunate lifestyle. They had only each other. This mutual caring was pointed out to them time and again and was the foundation for a satisfactory agreement."

In other situations, controversies between apartment mates may turn on interpretations of real estate law. In New York City many rental units are being converted to cooperative apartments. When unmarried adults live together, who has the right to buy the apartment? What if the person who signed the lease has moved out but now wants to be recognized as the official tenant? Whatever their rights may be against the landlord, the tenants may have a complex legal quarrel between themselves. In some cases, the solution may be complicated by emotional overlays.

• *Premarital agreements.* For most modern couples, the liabilities of marriage are accepted without much thought. One of the peculiarities of our society is the casual way in which people get married but how contentious they become when they are getting divorced.

Now, with increasing numbers of women working, we see a tendency toward prudent premarital planning. By negotiating a premarital agreement, the parties can protect their interests. Third persons may be affected, perhaps children from an earlier marriage. In helping to negotiate such an agreement, a family mediator with expertise in financial planning or tax problems can be particularly useful.

• *Agreements during a marriage.* Married couples may want to allocate their property for some private purpose. An impartial expert can help them work out the terms.

A case of this kind came to the Divorce and Child Custody Mediation Service in San Diego. The husband and wife were in their thirties; they were upper middle class, with two children, aged three and six, and had been married eleven years. He had a professional practice. She had not worked since the children's birth. They wanted to divide their assets to compensate her for homemaking and eventually to make it possible for each of them to be financially independent.

Mediator Faye Girsh handled the case. Girsh is a clinical psychologist who specializes in family counseling. Her primary role was to make sure that both parties were satisfied with the terms of the agreement.

The settlement was unique. The marital property was split to give the wife the equivalent of the salary and benefits she would have received in her former job. This came to $200,000, or about half of the joint assets. The real estate would remain in joint tenancy. The wife would be paid a prospective salary of $40,000 a year for five years. She could spend that money for education, for babysitting, or for anything else. After five years, she would return to work. All assets were allocated. The parties would jointly support the children, bargaining as to any expenditures that seemed excessive. They would consult about vacations, entertainment costs, and similar matters.

This mediation took six hours. It cost $450, with an additional two hours for a tax attorney, who charged $300.

• *Disagreements between homosexual partners.* A public court may not be an acceptable place to resolve such issues, but the individuals need help. Mediation may provide an appropriate answer, particularly if the mediator is sympathetic to alternate lifestyles.

One such case involved a valuable art collection that had been assembled by two men during the many years of their relationship. Now they were breaking up. Their friendship had been such that no records were available to show which man had paid for which pictures. A mediator helped them devise a blind auction that resolved their problem.

• *Disagreements between teenagers and their parents.* Quarrels between adolescents and their parents often concern the sharing of household or educational expenses. Disputes about the use of a family automobile can be particularly troublesome. Controversies involving an adolescent sometimes involve misbehavior by the child: running away, staying out of school, stealing money, or using drugs. A parent may decide to take such a child to court. In New York State, parents can have a child declared a PINS, a "person in need of supervision." Such children are called "status offenders." Similar court procedures are available in other jurisdictions. In appropriate cases, the court may be empowered to remove the child from the home for placement in an institution but, more likely, after a hearing the child is put on probation. This approach seldom cures the underlying problem.

Of course, if the child has broken the law, it may be difficult to stay out of court. And some judges think that even misbehavior should be dealt with in court. For example, Judge Don W. Reader of Canton, Ohio, has said that status offenders should be treated in the same way as juvenile delinquents: "Someone ought to have authority to say this isn't acceptable behavior in our community. Are you going to let him live out there in the street until he commits a crime?" But most authorities are skeptical about having courts handle such situations. Family courts and juvenile offender facilities are often overburdened, inadequate to the tasks they already must perform. It would be foolhardy to increase their purview.

Many delinquent children come from single-parent families, already suffering from poverty and stress. In the words of one social worker, "It is tough enough to live with most adolescents. When you are poor and overwhelmed by other aspects of your life, there comes a time when you need some help." Mediation can be a relatively inexpensive yet highly effective remedy here, as in any other family.

By engaging a family mediator, parents can deal directly with difficulties in the parent-child relationship, and an understanding can be reached about future behavior. However, parents should pull together. In discussions with the child, the parents should present a common front. One parent may try to impose discipline. If the other undercuts that effort, the first parent may give up or become overly strict. Dr. Donald A. Bloch, of the Ackerman Institute for Family Therapy, explains that "a split between the parents actually fuels the child's rule-breaking behavior. This kind of tug-of-war over a child is a major contribution to family disturbance."

A child's behavior may disrupt the relationship between the parents. In order to clear up their own problem, the parents may have to call a truce with their child. By isolating whatever aspects of the child's behavior are unacceptable and by coordinating their efforts, parents can begin to draft a set of rules that the child will accept. In effect, the parents and the child should negotiate a behavioral agreement. By exchanging promises, they can create an acceptable relationship for their future. Whether or not they actually use a mediator, they can reach a fair compromise by asking themselves what a third person would recommend. Then the parents should hold the child to the contract. Love and discipline go together.

Gary Friedman, a lawyer from Mill Valley, California, told me about one of his cases. A client came to him to see what could be done about keeping his twenty-one-year-old daughter from dissipating her inheritance on drugs and liquor. Friedman suggested that the father's "winning" such a case might have a bad effect on the daughter. Agreeing to act as a mediator, Friedman worked with the parties during five sessions. A mutual arrangement was concluded under which the daughter agreed to seek therapeutic help, to keep track of her finances, and to go back to college if her father would promise to stay out of her life. After five years, the parties were able to rebuild their relationship. The father is "off my back"; the daughter has "straightened out." They can see each other without squabbling.

Friedman contrasts this result with what often happens in court, where cases "seem to escalate almost automatically into legal wars marked by aggressiveness, righteousness, and hostility."

Dr. Derek Miller, director of an adolescent program in Chicago, says that many troubled kids are just "hanging around the house, waiting for love to turn up." Parents should not kick such a child out of their home. That may be exactly the wrong thing to do. A poem by Robert Frost, "The Death of the Hired Man," makes the point:

> Home is the place where, when you have to go there,
> They have to take you in.

By abandoning a child, the parents destroy their one opportunity to resolve the family's problems. Mediation is exactly the opposite. It encourages face-to-face discussion so that mutual understanding can take place.

An agency called Spectrum runs a youth shelter in Burlington, Vermont. My friend John Bourland, while working there, was asked to counsel a teenage runaway, Skip. When Bourland talked to him at the shelter, Skip was worried about his father's being angry. He was correct. Skip's father told Bourland on the phone that he planned to drag Skip back and give him a beating. Bourland drove to the parents' home. He asked them what they wanted from their son. As they talked, Bourland realized that Skip and his parents once had enjoyed a close family relationship. Unfortunately, the family had lost the knack of showing their mutual love and working out day-to-day problems. Bourland consequently warned the family that they needed to improve their ability to communicate. He recommended family therapy. Skip was willing to return home if a better relationship could be achieved. The father agreed not to punish the boy. By serving as an informal mediator, Bourland was able to bring the family together.

There are no easy answers to teenage behavioral problems. Every family must find its own way through the troubled adolescent years. Sometimes a thoughtful mediator may be helpful. It is a good sign when parents learn that it is possible to settle disputes without getting angry. Laughter and love don't hurt either.

• *Disputes involving students, teachers, administrators, and parents.* While working as a guidance counselor, Bourland was assigned another case. Public law mandates that every student receive necessary educational services. For students who qualify, appropriate special services must be provided by the school district. Since these services can be expensive, they often create disputes between parents and school officials. The local school principal asked Bourland to participate in a conference with a mother who was insisting that her son was "learning disabled" and therefore eligible to receive special services. The school said that the boy did not qualify because he was not trying hard enough. The school would not make any concessions, and the mother threatened to go to court.

At this point, Bourland talked privately with the mother. She believed that her son needed extra help. She didn't really care how assistance was provided. Bourland then explored various alternatives with the administrators. They were willing to allow the student to participate in a less expensive remedial program. The offer was accepted by the mother. In a joint session, a plan was drawn up and litigation was avoided. Mediation had solved the problem.

• *Teenage pregnancies.* Difficult questions arise in this situation. Is marriage a possibility? Does the girl want an abortion? If the baby is brought to term, how should responsibility for child care be allocated? Should the baby be put up for adoption? These decisions involve the rights and responsibilities of various members of the family, including the putative father. In some situations, a mediator can help a family decide such questions in a less emotional atmosphere than might otherwise prevail.

If the girl decides to keep her child, it will be necessary to make arrangements for its support. In some cases, the father may agree to bear some of the burden. Otherwise her parents may have to provide help. Obviously, it would be better for all concerned if such questions could be resolved privately.

Often the girl will decide to put her child up for adoption. Adoptions are regulated by law. When placement is arranged by an agency, the natural mother may never know the identity of the adoptive parents. Even if she changes her mind about the adoption, it will be difficult for her to reclaim the child. When an adoption is approved, a judge must determine whether it will benefit the child. If the family has been selected by an agency, the necessary legalities will have been observed: the parents or the guardian of the child will have consented to the adoption; in most jurisdictions, adoption records are sealed and will not be made available either to the natural parents or to the child.

In private placements, the identity of the adoptive parents is more likely to surface. Then there is a risk that the natural mother may try to regain custody of her child. If the formalities were not observed, the adoption may be susceptible to attack. If a court decides that the consent was involuntary, the adoption may be annulled. Extraneous issues may arise. A decision may turn on whether there was a sufficient number of witnesses to the original consent agreement. A family court has to deal with those kinds of technicalities, and a judge has only a few moments to focus on each matter. Sometimes the child's welfare gets lost in the legalities.

If the natural mother and the adopting couple are concerned about the child, such a dispute may be appropriate for mediation. The parties can negotiate an arrangement for the child. An impartial mediator can encourage the parties to concentrate upon the best interests of the child.

• *Disputes over proposed moves.* The interests of various members of the family may have to be accommodated when a job promotion entails relocation. Here, too, mediation may be helpful. A rising executive received a promotion that required a transfer from Connecticut to Kansas. Everyone else in the family was upset. One son would have to leave the local high school. Another son was at college in Massachusetts. The daughter had recently taken a job in New York. The mother refused to leave Connecticut until everyone was satisfied with the move. For several months, the father lived in a hotel near his new office, traveling to Connecticut every weekend to discuss the family's problem. For a time, a marital separation seemed inevitable. The situation was successfully resolved when a family friend agreed to act as a mediator.

• *Problems associated with retirement.* Family expenditures may have to be reduced when a working family member retires. A neutral adviser can help family members accept such changes and encourage them to readjust their lifestyle.

Decisions about home care or institutionalization for elderly parents can be particularly troublesome. Necessary trade-offs between members of the family can be mediated.

• *Disputes over inheritance.* Probate lawyers dread such situations. Families can embark upon lifetime feuds. By having to take sides, the dear old family lawyer may become a pariah with one branch of the family. Mediation can eliminate the need for litigation.

• *Disagreements over family businesses.* Which member of the family will control the firm? How is income to be allocated? Rather than take such problems to court, ask a neutral expert to mediate the dispute. Many closely held corporations include dispute-settlement procedures in their bylaws: disputes are to be resolved through arbitration or with help from a neutral mediator.

• *Violence between relatives.* Dianne Simmons of the Neighborhood Justice Center of Honolulu sent me a case that involved two members of an extended family who had gotten into a fight at a wedding. One man's arm was broken. His mother was insulted. He was prepared to file formal charges but was persuaded, for the good of the family, to mediate. An agreement was worked out that included payment of his medical expenses and an apology to his mother. Both sides were pleased to settle the matter out of court because they did not want to split the family.

America is violent, particularly when families and lovers are involved. Alcohol releases whatever inhibitions might restrain them. After a few drinks, the "defensive" handguns are snatched out of bedside tables. All too frequently family members turn up dead at the local morgue. No wonder cops don't like to break up family fights. It is too much to ask that a mediator step into the line of fire, but if some of the problems could have been resolved in advance, many of these family fights need never have occurred.

As mediation becomes widely accepted, it will be used to resolve a wide range of family controversies. There is no sign that such disputes will diminish. If anything, they are likely to increase. Widespread unemployment and reduced social services will put even more pressure on American families. On Mother's Day, 1982, a coalition of

national women's organizations sent President Reagan the
following telegram:

> The budget cuts proposed by the President have a devastating
> impact on women and their families at every stage of their
> lives. For women who head their families, it will mean a faster
> decline into deeper poverty; it will mean less child care, less
> nutritional assistance, fewer health services. For women who
> are abandoned by their husbands, it will mean reduced possi-
> bilities for job training, less support for their children's edu-
> cation, and greater difficulty in getting legal services.

The economic recession is bearing down on the American family. Litigation would make things even worse. In
contrast, family mediation can strengthen the family.

How did family mediation get started?

Family mediation was first used by religious groups. The
church or synagogue often gets involved in family disputes,
not always, of course, as a mediator.

Local parish priests, rabbis, and ministers frequently
talk with warring couples, encouraging them to resolve
their problems. In 1920, the Jewish community in New
York City established a conciliation board that is still in
operation. Even earlier, the Chinese Benevolent Association provided mediation. Settlement houses continue to
offer a similar service.

In the late 1960s, social workers noticed that increasing
numbers of family disputes were going to court. People
were turning to government because they had nowhere else
to go. They had lost touch with the voluntary agencies. In
the early 1970s, the American Arbitration Association held
a meeting that brought together some of the pioneers in the
field of family mediation, including the late O. J. Coogler,
Sheila Kessler, and Mark Lohman. According to *American
Family* (1981), "This meeting contributed greatly to the
momentum of the mediation movement." Social agencies

recognized that mediation represented a fundamental change in how families could be helped. Mediation made it possible to encourage families to resolve their own disputes. This was an attractive idea.

One executive director put it this way: "If mediation works, I can see our agency giving it a high priority. We believe that a trained mediator can help people manage their own problems. If we can teach our clients to settle disputes on their own, they will be better off. Any time you can keep a kid out of court, you are on the right track."

Family therapists were intrigued. Many people are reluctant to enter therapy for fear of being considered crazy, but when a family therapist serves as a mediator the clients are not under treatment. No problem. Therapists have been critical of family courts. They believe that courts are overburdened and caught up in the law. "Litigation is destructive of family values." Mediation is different because it provides an opportunity to strengthen the family. Therapists like that: One told me that "the way agreement is reached can be equally as important as the agreement itself." Therapists are excited by mediation because it gives them a chance to restructure the parties' attitude toward their life. While working on a dispute, a therapist can bring about positive behavioral shifts.

What is a mediator supposed to accomplish?

The immediate goal is to help people resolve a particular dispute. The ultimate purpose is to give them confidence and control over their own lives. Clients are encouraged to become independent.

In divorce, parties need to abandon the empty shell of their former marriage and set forth on a new, independent life. They must learn how to live alone, no longer depending upon their prior relationship. If they have children, they need to provide a sensible regime for their care.

In other family disputes, the parties must learn to accept a family structure without becoming its slave. A mediator can help people to explore their needs and cope with their anger, while reaffirming their mutual obligations and their love. In the process, each person will achieve rediscovery. The final settlement may not be as important as the exploration. Mediation provides an opportunity to learn how to deal with the frustrations that accompany any family relationship.

Lori Eisenberg, director of the Center for Separation and Divorce Mediation in Falls Church, Virginia, became interested in mediation through a couple she attempted to help as a family counselor. She had encouraged them to seek legal advice about getting a divorce. In short order, the couple's friendship was destroyed by the bitterness of the adversarial process. Soon after the wife consulted an attorney, he jacked up her initial demands for child support. When the husband's lawyer took over the bargaining, the parties no longer were permitted to speak to each other. The husband lost all contact with the children. He was advised to withhold support. The wife took the children out of school and moved to another state. It was a devastating experience. Eisenberg signed up for training in mediation with the late O. J. Coogler. Since then she has dedicated her career to guiding families through a divorce. Eisenberg wrote to me about a recent mediation:

> My clients were referred by the psychiatrist who was treating the husband. They had agreed to seek a divorce and wanted to maintain friendly relations while they settled the remaining details. Our first two-hour session was uneventful. They had filled out financial statements. Everything was proceeding smoothly. Only during the discussion of the husband's pension benefits did a flare-up of concealed resentment briefly surface and quickly subside.
>
> I next met with their two children, ages thirteen and sixteen, to explore their preference as to which parent the children wanted to live with. To my surprise, each child expressed

ignorance of the fact that their parents were separating. They had not been aware of any problems. When I brought both parents in with the children to discuss the children's confusion, the quietly rational mother exploded. She ventilated her bitterness about what had gone wrong in her marriage. She had never expected her husband to ask for divorce.

The next session began with everyone present and silent. All of my skills were necessary if I was to heal the wounds in this family, not deepen them. I chose to start the session with preparing a family map—a nonthreatening way to unfold the family history. Mother and father sat next to each other—father smiling, mother grim.

The father disclosed how he dealt with disappointment, how he had learned not to talk about feelings, how he had learned to deal with conflict by withdrawal, going his own way. Then it was the mother's turn to describe her family: an alcoholic father, poverty, the children and mother banding together to help each other, learning not to make demands because that would mean greater hardship for the mother. I asked the father how he handled his feelings when his wife was critical. There it was. He withdrew into work, into activities, and finally to other women who expected less. The children sat silent. Now it was the mother's turn to describe her feelings in the marriage, her hopes, her disappointments, her way of handling her feelings, her mounting blame from which the father constantly withdrew. She cried about the divorce. Her daughter came to her side. Her son looked angrily at the floor. Father cleared his throat, "I know I never learned to discuss things, to talk about things. That's why I'm in therapy now. But I want you to know this so we can talk, so you can ask questions, so you can understand more than I did, so you'll have a better chance to work things out than I did."

It was time for the children to understand that this separation had nothing to do with them, that each of their parents loved and would continue to love them. I quietly summed up for the children their parents' journey—what they had learned or hadn't learned about a loving marriage and how they, the children, in seeing their parents as people, could learn to love them and know they needn't lose either of them and learn more of what they needed for themselves, now and in their future relationships. The end of the session was not a happy one. It was silent and sad. I didn't know of the doors that had been opened, only the sadness of what had unfolded.

In ensuing sessions, the couple's separation was arranged. This family did regain an ability to communicate. The children could be open with their parents. According to Eisenberg, the process not only resolved the legal issues but also provided an opportunity for her clients to gain a better understanding of their relationships and to preserve some respect and concern for each other.

Does a mediator deal with the parties' emotions?

A mediator is not a therapist, but a mediator should understand that parties are likely to be under stress and may be feeling grief, despair, depression, or loneliness. Parties may feel that they have failed; they may have lost confidence in themselves. In a family dispute, emotional pressure can be overwhelming. Watch out for it. Parties who are incapable of negotiating should not be in mediation.

Strong feelings are present in many family controversies. In a divorce, feelings can be particularly intense. Even in an ordinary family quarrel, emotions may suddenly erupt. Clients may storm out of the room after screaming at each other and at the mediator.

A mediator may encounter all of the following reactions and more:

- *Anger.* When family members can't get what they want, they may lash out at anyone who seems to be in their way. They see themselves as victimized.

- *Guilt.* Anger and guilt go hand in hand, reinforcing each other. We are told not to be angry at people we love. In frustration, we convert our anger into guilt which creates more anger. Now our rage takes command. We discover that we are completely out of control.

* *Alienation.* Powerlessness leads to further frustration. Most people find an identity within their family. When family members lose the ability to influence each other, they become alienated. A father who has lost custody may feel that he no longer has control over his children. This may make it easier to abandon the children.

* *Inadequacy.* The loss of family may threaten a person's sense of identity. Loneliness and self-doubt color the world grey. The self-acknowledged victim of a family controversy may indulge in self-pity. Cut off from the family, this individual may drift into lonely self-indulgence, wondering how to punish whoever seems responsible.

A family can be an important source of strength. Loss of family can be devastating, particularly when an individual is already worrying about finances, finding a new social life, fulfilling sexual needs, and taking care of the children. Mediators should be alert to such concerns; they should try to resolve the dispute without generating unnecessary guilt or anger and to put the parties in touch with appropriate resources.

Mediators must work through the parties. In some systems of dispute settlement, the parties give over decision-making power to a professional advocate. Not so in mediation. The mediator must be particularly sensitive about how the parties' emotions are likely to affect the positions they take in the negotiations.

Psychotherapist Marsha Dorsky, who mediates in New York City, has described such a case. The parties came to her several years after their divorce. Their separation agreement included an arbitration clause, but the arbitrator had encouraged them to mediate a dispute about their son's education.

The husband had remarried and moved away. He was unhappy about the school his son was attending. When the parties talked with Dorsky, she noted their hostility toward each other. The initial session was permeated with jealousy ("You are turning the child against me") and accusations ("The child has problems because of you"). The dispute gave the father an opportunity to gain power over the child. Once their hostility had surfaced, Dorsky encouraged the parties to compromise. At her suggestion, each parent submitted a list of three schools that would be acceptable. Then, in separate sessions, each of them eliminated one school from the list. They agreed to file applications with the four remaining schools for the next semester. Dorsky suggested that if more than one opening became available, their son should make the final choice. The couple agreed.

As it turned out, none of the schools had an opening, but the parties were able to agree upon another school that did. By gaining insight into why the parties were fighting so bitterly over the school issue, the mediator was able to suggest a formula for resolving the impasse. The father really wanted to reassert some control over his son's life. The mother was afraid that any school the father selected might be too liberal, that he "wanted to make the child into a hippie." Encouraged to compromise, the parents were able to agree upon a conventional school.

Why not ask an arbitrator to decide?

Mediation is one option for resolving disputes. There are other ways to encourage negotiation.

• *Arbitration*. In arbitration, an impartial third person is asked to decide the issue. The decision may be final and binding. Some families are willing to submit to impartial arbitration but many people want to make their own settlement. No third party can know as much about the situation as the parties themselves. I do not recommend arbitration in family disputes until all attempts to negotiate the problem have failed. Arbitration may be preferable to going to court, particularly if the arbitrator is someone the parties trust. But I am firmly convinced that an amicable settlement is the best solution.

Arbitration clauses in contracts assure that disputes that may arise in the future will be decided without going to court. Arbitration clauses often appear in separation agreements. Then, as changes take place in the family environment, adjustments can more easily be made. First the parties should try to agree. Usually such problems can be worked out informally. If the parties are unable to agree, they can refer the issue to an arbitrator. The arbitrator can be an expert on family law, a social worker, or any other kind of expert. The American Arbitration Association's rules for arbitrating separation agreements are printed in Appendix B of this book. They have been tested in court and are well accepted by practicing attorneys.

• *Advisory opinions.* When parties are unable to agree but don't want an arbitrator to make a final and binding decision, they can ask a neutral expert to recommend a solution. Such an opinion may be based upon an independent investigation, upon discussions with the parties, or upon a formal hearing. Sometimes advisory opinions are requested by family courts. In other cases, the parties' attorneys may agree that such an opinion is necessary. Before agreeing to such a procedure, parties should ask themselves: What is the effect of such an opinion? Are the parties likely to abide by it?

• *Mediation-Arbitration.* A neutral person may attempt to mediate a dispute but be given authority to decide any issues that the parties are unable to settle. This person may then conduct hearings and issue a binding decision. In short, the process combines voluntary mediation and binding arbitration. Some community mediation centers use a version of this approach.

Why isn't it a good idea to go to court?

Court litigation is the government's way to decide disputes, and plenty of family arguments do end up in court. Domestic relations cases have doubled over the past decade. Indeed, the bulk of civil cases filed in court involve family disputes.

Litigation can be time-consuming, expensive, and traumatic. Witnesses must reveal humiliating details about their personal lives. The atmosphere of a court can be oppressive and threatening. People find the experience degrading. The bitterness of lawsuits can create family feuds that persist for generations.

On the other hand, the possibility of a lawsuit may be the motivating force that makes bargaining a realistic option. A husband may be content to continue living at home long after his marriage is dead. Only a threatened lawsuit will induce him to face the issues in a more reasonable way.

Without access to the courts, many family members would be out of luck. Thus, mediation depends upon the judicial process. At the same time, it provides an attractive alternative in many cases, an opportunity for people who are sensible enough to use it. Mediation will never eliminate the need for effective family courts but can relieve the courts of many unnecessary cases.

A description of family court procedure is beyond the scope of this book. Bear in mind that if a lawsuit becomes necessary, the parties will need attorneys who are experienced in this area of the law. Most lawsuits are settled out of court by the attorneys rather than at trial. Unfortunately, even those that are settled out of court often require extensive discovery procedures, during which the lawyers jockey for position. Once a family turns a dispute over to opposing lawyers, it may be too late to negotiate a friendly settlement.

Do lawyers prevent settlement?

I would not put it that bluntly. Most lawyers work hard to negotiate for their clients. The adversary process itself is what presents problems. Each lawyer is expected to obtain everything possible for the client. This approach may poison an already troubled relationship. Smoldering resentment may burst into destructive flames.

Financial considerations are likely to be emphasized by divorce lawyers at the expense of continuing family relationships. Lawyers try to "beat" the other party. They seldom bring a family together to discuss common problems. Harvard law professor Frank E. A. Sander believes that the lawyer's first advice is likely to be: "Above all, don't talk to your spouse." Sander should know. He is an authority on domestic relations law.

Lawyers believe that they are obligated to speak for their clients. It might be unethical for them to do otherwise. Many lawyers think that the adversary process stands in the way of amicable settlements. Patricia Kane, a lawyer who runs the divorce mediation program in Old Greenwich, Connecticut, explains it this way: "People can rarely negotiate a divorce by themselves. When they take the legal route, they experience a loss of control. Lawyers take over and they are left out of the process, producing much of the stress, bitterness, confusion, and aftershock that often accompany an adversarial proceeding."

Professionals like to work within familiar systems. The adversary process seems comfortable, although some lawyers express concern about the pain and discomfort that they encounter in contested divorce proceedings.

The late O. J. Coogler was particularly critical of di-

vorce lawyers, as becomes clear from a passage from
Structured Mediation in Divorce Settlements (1979):

> Lawyers, like undertakers, are presumed to have the answer
> to questions in their field, but unlike undertakers, lawyers
> never answer the questions. The one thing the client is very
> sure of from the consultation is that it is all very hard to un-
> derstand. From this follows a decision to leave it up to the
> lawyer who then compliments the client for having made a
> wise choice as a check for the retainer fee is written. . . . Once
> a second attorney is employed, the only factor limiting esca-
> lation of the competitive struggle between husband and wife is
> the financial resources of the family. In some cases, the strug-
> gle may continue not just through the divorce, but for the
> lifetime of the parties.

In my opinion, Coogler should not have cast divorce lawyers as the villains. Many attorneys recognize that the adversary process inhibits their ability to satisfy the needs of
the family. Because of the problems that clients encounter
in family litigation, attorneys encourage them to settle.
They understand that mediation offers a way to avoid the
courts.

As Professor Sander warns his students, "The adversary process is not appropriate for most family controversies." Many lawyers would agree, but were never taught
to mediate. Only a few law schools give courses on negotiation, mediation, or arbitration. And these courses tend
to focus on labor relations.

In a 1982 article in the *Ohio State Law Journal,* Professor Leonard L. Riskin, of the University of Houston Law
Center, argues that training lawyers to mediate would lead
to greater use of this approach: "The spread of mediation
could do much to improve the quality of life in our society
. . . because it fosters interaction among people and em-
powers them to control their own lives" (p. 57). Other law
professors are coming to the same conclusion. As we will
see in subsequent chapters, many lawyers recognize the
need for mediation services.

Some lawyers do incite controversy. Sybil Anne Davis,

who heads the Family Law Section of the Los Angeles County Bar Association, remembers that when she began practicing law it was customary for the husband's lawyer to

> make a wife come to her knees financially. Cut off support. Take all the money out of the bank. Don't make the mortgage payments. Don't pay the utility bills. Cancel all her credit cards. Leave her stranded without any money. And then threaten to take the kids away from her, not because you want them but to get her to cave in and give up more property. That's how the game was played and it still is by certain lawyers who feel the only way to be a lawyer is to be an aggressive son-of-a-bitch!

Davis refuses to get involved in vindictive child custody battles and is delighted by California's recently passed presumption for joint custody: "You don't lose your right to be a parent just because of a divorce. The kids don't have to lose a mother or father either." She supports mediation: "It goes back to my belief that you are better off if you control your own destiny, rather than have a court make a ruling for you."

Conclusion

This chapter introduces family mediation, explaining how it can help families to resolve their disputes. Best known for its use in facilitating marital separations, mediation can also be used in a wide variety of situations within families. A mediator is not a judge. To the contrary, a family mediator tries to help the parties adopt a positive approach toward their differences. A mediator must be fair to both parties. Based on experience with similar cases, the mediator must demonstrate an ability to bring about solid and enforceable settlements. Some of the necessary skills of mediators are outlined. Finally, the advantages of family

mediation over court litigation are demonstrated. Since the
benefits of creating a working relationship between the parties are stressed, mediation can be less disruptive for a
family than going to court.

2

Family Mediation in Action

IN COMMERCIAL NEGOTIATIONS, firms are represented by people with equivalent levels of competence. Since this is seldom the case in family disputes, family mediators find a ready market for their skills.

The purpose of this chapter is to illustrate how mediation works. It first explains how to negotiate. Bargaining can occur in many different settings, with or without mediators. The skills are transferable. But within a family, bargaining occurs in a unique setting. Family disputes are intensely personal. The adversaries are not dealing with organizations but with individuals, people who never expected to confront each other at a bargaining table.

In many cases, family members have been avoiding the problem, refusing to confront the disagreement that must be dealt with. Often, some explosive event must occur before the adversaries realize that their life cannot go on as it has. Perhaps an act of violence: one couple decided that they had to get a divorce in the aftermath of a drunken quarrel that ended with them wrestling on the kitchen floor. Another couple turned to mediation after their teenage son threw all of the parents' clothes out of the front door and locked himself in his room. Then it was time to talk. But how?

Don't most people already know how to negotiate?

Schools don't teach children how to negotiate. Decisions tend to be made unilaterally by teachers or administrators, without the students being asked to participate in the process.

I asked some educators why this was so. Wallace M. Lornell, an assistant commissioner in the New York State Education Department, explained: "Your comment that students are seldom instructed in the skills of negotiating or mediation or arbitration is true. Many educators are of the opinion that the specific skill of negotiating is included in the social growth process."

Children's lack of exposure to the negotiating process may explain their alienation from school activities and their subsequent negative attitudes toward society. If students are not encouraged to take charge of their own lives, one can hardly blame them for losing interest.

Some teachers do provide such training. When teachers understand mediation, they may be willing to import those skills into the classroom. If children could be persuaded to solve their problems with words rather than with force, many of the current frustrations in the school environment might be eliminated. Dr. John Kastan of the Council on Children and Families of New York State agrees: "So often, youth and adults resort to violence because of an inability to express and articulate their points of view, as well as an unwillingness to understand what others are saying."

By creating an internal mediation program, involving students as well as teachers, a school could strengthen students' capacity to cope with many behavioral problems. Mediation training promotes responsibility and good citizenship.

Commissioner Lornell again: "There is no doubt that family relationships need to be strengthened in our society and that people who develop negotiating skills make a contribution to this effort. Certainly, teachers and other educators should be encouraged to help students recognize and respect the rights of other people, to speak out forcefully for a point of view and to be tolerant of the other person's viewpoint."

On the other hand, Lornell does not think that a specific course on negotiating is necessary. Garrett W. Murphy, director of the New York State Education Department's Division for Continuing Education, says that the elementary curriculum already includes enough material on negotiating skills, particularly in the areas of communications and social studies. "Getting to know each other, listening to others' concerns, and showing a willingness to compromise are the cornerstone of negotiation. This interaction with people is an integral part of the elementary school."

I am not sure that social studies courses provide an adequate introduction to negotiating and mediating. As Dr. Kastan explained in a letter to me: "The history that is glorified most often is that of wars, debates, and charismatic autocrats, rather than peaceful settlements." I think he is correct when he says that

in order for negotiating to be taken seriously by students, several changes may be needed in the schools. Most obviously, there would need to be trained instructors in substantial numbers available, for I imagine these techniques are not currently familiar to most teachers. More significantly, the social system of the school might need to be altered, as negotiation is not the traditional means of dispute settlement among students, teachers, and administrators. Careful study of the implications

of introducing negotiation into the schools would provide most
interesting findings.

Of course, as Dr. David S. Seeley, the author of *Education Through Partnership* and former director of the
Public Education Association, warned me in a recent letter: "It would take considerable effort and resources to
train school teachers to instruct their students in these
skills. Such training, however, might have a side benefit of
enabling teachers themselves to do a better job of negotiating. . . . Classrooms and schools run on a partnership
basis may provide more practice in negotiation for both
teacher and student than those run on a bureaucratic
basis." Seeley is also wary of establishing a "separate curriculum, or time away from academic learning, since there
are already so many distractions from this main function of
the schools."

An excerpt from a letter to me from Cynthia Parsons,
the education editor of the *Christian Science Monitor,*
drives that point into the flesh:

> Schools have an overriding business . . . and they have a great
> deal of trouble sticking to that business with all the good sug-
> gestions from folks like you who want them to teach health,
> sexual understanding, how to drive a car, when and how to
> smoke and drink, how to make aprons and bookends, and how
> to negotiate in human relation stress situations. The overriding
> business of the schools is to teach children how to read, write,
> and compute . . . how to do and appreciate both the fine and
> practical arts.

Most adults have not been trained in negotiating skills.
In fact, there is not much likelihood that teachers will ever
receive such training. Educators seem content to continue
spooning out the traditional curriculum. In many school
systems, negotiating is a dirty word: it sounds like organiz-
ing a union. In fact, people negotiate every day but don't
realize that they are negotiating. And they have vague
ideas about mediation. As a first order of business, a family

mediator must always explain the process to the parties. Never assume that people understand it.

When he was working as director of alternative education for a public high school, John Bourland dealt with many students who are experiencing difficulty in school:

> They are generally belligerent or withdrawn in their reaction to authority, impulsive and apathetic. A major reason for this is that they do not know how to negotiate with others. They are ruled by their emotions and react impulsively to pressure situations. In our programs, they are taught to negotiate through role-play, group discussion, and formal instruction. Students are encouraged to deal with a variety of issues, working with the staff.

Bourland believes that learning negotiating skills helps students manage their lives better. The process involves a change in both behavior and perception, best achieved by exposing students to appropriate role models. Accordingly, he encourages teachers and administrators to add negotiating skills to their repertoire.

The executive director of Advocates for Children, Miriam Thompson, wrote me that mediation strategies have proved useful in her agency's efforts to pursue "policy changes in the school system that will benefit children," but, as she warns, "If we teach children these skills, we must make sure that the school supports a climate and structure for their application and execution."

What does a mediator do?

The mediator's task is to help the parties reach a settlement. First, the mediator must be sure that the parties know what they want to accomplish. Can they picture their future life realistically? Do they have a general plan of action?

When the parties understand what they want and seem willing to make some concessions, the mediator can begin to work with them. The mediator helps them identify areas of agreement and disagreement. Once this is done, the parties can begin to negotiate toward a solution. The result of successful mediation is the key to their future.

"It sounds so easy," one mediator scolded me. "Don't give people the impression that family mediation is a breeze. Most couples can't even talk to each other. They hate themselves and each other. They are stuck at that level. Logic isn't going to move them. They have to see it themselves. Mediators must expect that many times they will fail." To quote New York mediator Adriane Berg: "Real mediators sweat."

How does mediation begin?

At the first meeting, the mediator explains exactly what the parties should expect. They should be given a chance to ask questions. They must understand both the limitations of the process and the preliminary work that must be done before negotiations can begin.

It is important that the parties participate in the process voluntarily. They may come to the first meeting without any real commitment. There is much misunderstanding. Some people think that a mediator is a judge. One of the parties may have been pressured into coming. The mediator should explain that mediation is entirely voluntary, that the mediator can merely assist the parties in reaching an agreement. It may be helpful to warn about the strong likelihood of failure. The mediator should be certain that the parties understand the heavy burden they must assume.

Henry M. Elson, a Berkeley, California, attorney-mediator, reports that about a third of his clients drop out of mediation after the first or second session. Only half continue to an agreement.

At the first meeting, many family mediators give the couple a written explanation of the process. California mediator Isolina Ricci uses a one-page document that explains how mediation differs from counseling and from arbitration. The handout states that the mediator will help the parties identify certain issues and agree upon ground rules. The mediator will guide the parties through a series of meetings and assist them in selecting a formula for their future life. The parties are assured that the sessions will be confidential. Ricci also tells the parties exactly what to expect from the mediator.

Some aspects of Ricci's approach are unique.

- What is said by one party is communicated to the other party. She will not keep secrets.

- The parties must authorize her to discuss the negotiations with each of their attorneys. From time to time, she will talk with the lawyers on the telephone, keeping them informed.

- She will help the parties write up those parts of their agreement that relate to parenting rights and responsibilities. Agreements as to support or property must be drafted by the couple's attorneys. Ricci is not a lawyer.

- She refuses to take sides. It is understood that she will not testify in court. Her allegiance is to the family, not to any individual family member.

- Ricci makes no mention of arbitration. If the parties are unable to agree, the mediation is over. The parents can seek a solution elsewhere.

What happens if one party refuses to participate?

Mediation is voluntary. If one person refuses to participate, mediation does not take place.

The threat of compelling someone to appear in court initiates many negotiations, most notably in divorce cases. Typically, one of the parties will have to take some drastic action to convince the other that divorce is inevitable.

Some individuals are afraid to challenge the head of their family. Rather than do so, they try to avoid critical issues. They may run away from home or they may submit to that person's control. They can't stand the idea of a confrontation. Then negotiations are unlikely.

A person who believes that an adversary is powerless may see no reason to negotiate. To bring such a person to the bargaining table, pressure must be created.

In some families, the notion that a parent should bargain with a child may be unacceptable. Some parents assume that they can continue to dominate their children. A father may cut off a child without support or abandon his wife and children. Then it may be too late to negotiate. Again, in order to initiate discussion, the child or wife may have to take some drastic action, such as threatening to move out of the home.

At the other extreme, family members may be content to play a subservient role, unwilling to insist upon their rights. If people won't demand the right to negotiate, not much can be done. It is, after all, up to the worm to turn.

Some people can't establish enough of a relationship with others even to discuss their problems. These situations are becoming rare. In our culture, people love to express themselves. Most of us are able to bargain toward a reasonable compromise.

When parties come to a family mediator, they should realize that some changes will have to take place in their relationship. The mediator should ascertain whether they are serious about making concessions. One may still be stalling for time. At the first interview, the mediator must try to discover each person's attitude toward the negotiations.

Should there be a retainer agreement?

At the initial meeting between the mediator and the parties, they should reach an understanding. The role of the mediator has to be clarified. A sample agreement is included as Appendix D. This document establishes the mediator's relationship with the parties. It also protects the mediator against liability. An arrangement should be reached about fees. How much will be charged? When will the mediator be paid? How will the cost be allocated?

What is a typical mediation scenario?

When a mediator has been retained, it is time to create an operating agenda. Here is a checklist that indicates the sequence of events.

1. Establish a relationship with the parties, defining the mediator's role.

2. Design a schedule for the sessions that can be followed to conclusion.

3. Adopt a method for obtaining whatever information is required to understand the parties' problems.

4. Identify the various areas of agreement.

5. Define the issues that must be resolved.

6. Assist the parties in their negotiations.

7. Formulate a final settlement.

8. Arrange for the terms of the settlement to be transmitted to the attorneys for filing in court, if necessary.

In a sense, the mediator is hired as a consultant, jointly retained to help the parties work their way through the hazardous journey from impasse to resolution. The check-list shows the route to that final destination.

Although a family mediator does serve as an adviser to the parties, there is far more involved than simply providing information. A family mediator is like a consultant. The process can be described in terms of a consulting project. Putting that work in sequence, a mediator is expected to carry out the following tasks:

1. At the initial interview, the mediator and the parties should discuss the process to be sure that they fully understand their goals and the purpose of the mediation.

2. During the early stages of the mediation, the mediator must help the parties bring together the information they will need to understand their problem. The mediator will be expected to provide additional information and to raise questions that help identify and explore the needs of the family.

3. The parties will look to their mediator for practical solutions. Sometimes they may be unable to focus upon their real problem. It will be up to the mediator to ask them whether their trouble does not lie somewhere else. A mediator should be skeptical of the parties' initial version of their dispute. Otherwise, the parties may waste time attempting to deal with symptoms but fail to uncover the underlying cause of the family's problem. A mediator must be able to ask hard, seemingly impertinent questions without offending clients. When an impasse develops over the allocation of apparently valueless personal property, the mediator may conclude that important emotional concerns are blocking a resolution. A family dog, for example, may generate overwhelming emotional attachments.

4. The mediator must take time to diagnose the problem. This can prove frustrating to the parties. They may have to educate the mediator about their affairs in attempting to describe what went wrong with their relationship. When the parties participate in the diagnostic process, they are more likely to understand the need for a particular solution.

More than one client has complained that a mediator has become bogged down in what appears to be a tedious exploration of irrelevancies. "Let's get on with it," they say. "Our problem is simply to reach a practical arrangement for the future." At this point, the mediator may have to persuade the parties to continue the discussion. The mediator should raise some pertinent questions. Which areas do they seem hesitant to discuss? What unexpressed motivations might there be for avoiding such subjects? How willing are they to confront underlying problems?

Unless the parties see the mediator's efforts as building a momentum toward agreement, they may express renewed impatience.

Mediation is a collaborative activity. Unless the clients think that the mediator is following a sensible course, they may begin to reject further efforts to divert them from what they regard as the main points at issue.

It is up to the mediator to justify the time that may be required to understand fully the issues to be resolved. The mediator should point out the importance of reaching a sound solution. Unless the parties actually comply with the final agreement, it will not resolve their problems.

5. At some stage, the mediator may need to make a recommendation. Here, of course, the similarity with consulting disappears. A consultant's client can demand such an opinion. The family mediator has two or more clients and must be careful not to inhibit their efforts to come to an agreement. Still, a mediator may want to recommend an approach that involves process rather than substance. A mediator can identify what issues need to be decided but should not tell the parties how to decide them.

6. The mediator's proper role in implementing an agreement is debatable. Some mediators think that implementation should be left to the parties. Others think that the mediator is in the best position to monitor the parties' performance and should continue to work with the parties, serving as a referee or arbitrator as disputes arise in future

years. The scope of the mediator's later dealings with the parties preferably should be left up to them.

Some mediators believe that temporary arrangements should be implemented even while the final terms of an agreement are being worked out. For example, an interim regime as to custody or visitation can be put into effect while discussions continue. If the arrangement seems to work, this formula can be made a part of the final agreement.

7. An overall responsibility of the mediator is to facilitate the family's understanding of its unique situation, helping individual members to cope with future challenges. This aspect of mediation may represent its most lasting value but should not be stressed with clients. No one likes to be told that they are not competent to handle their own affairs, either as a parent or as a self-sufficient adult. To the extent that a mediator can accomplish behavioral modification, it should be done with circumspection.

How does a mediator obtain information from the parties?

A mediator must take time to understand the issues. The mediator may have to help with complex financial problems. A common technique is to require the parties to submit financial information. When both parties agree upon the facts, they are more likely to come to a mutually satisfactory solution.

No relevant information should be withheld. One party may attempt to hide assets. Another may neglect to mention certain property or fail to disclose a secret plan for the future. A mediator must ferret out such information. The more the mediator learns about the case, the less likely the mediator will be surprised.

Good advice from one mediator: "Don't be afraid to ask. You have to ask the right questions. One thing leads to another. Be alert. You must listen carefully. It is not that they lie to you, but they may not volunteer all of the information. You have to dig it out.''

To learn as much as possible about the case may involve asking a series of questions. In more complicated situations, such as a divorce, several sessions may be required to develop detailed information about the couple's assets and expenses and to test their expectations. Careful fact gathering will help the mediator learn what the dispute is about.

Both parties should be present during this phase. Later, the mediator's understanding can be augmented at separate sessions or by obtaining specially requested statements from the parties. The parties may not want to disclose certain information in each other's presence. The mediator must find a way to bring such information to the surface so that it can be shared.

In obtaining necessary information, the mediator will have to ask questions about the parties' personal history. The purpose is to help the parties reach an agreement for the future, not to rekindle past differences.

People involved in a family dispute are likely to be angry with each other, preoccupied with old scores. This is flagrantly so in a divorce. The mediator must get the parties to turn away from the past, to concentrate upon reaching a settlement. The past should be understood and then set aside. The parties must realize that their primary task is to design a new relationship.

During the negotiations, the mediator may need additional information about the parties' expenses and assets. A questionnaire can be helpful here. Likewise, asking each party to prepare a personal budget may disclose useful information and will encourage the parties to focus upon their future. Such an inventory will facilitate financial planning and help the parties establish goals and objectives for their subsequent bargaining. Unless both parties are aware of the available resources, they will not be able to negotiate realistically. The mediator must convince them that they will benefit from full disclosure.

When should a mediator call a recess?

Face-to-face negotiations are not always appropriate. If the discussions break down, a recess should be taken. The parties may need time to reflect, to cool off, or to discuss their bargaining strategy with outsiders. The mediator should be aware that the parties often will want to talk with friends or even with other professionals. This should be encouraged. Sometimes a proposal needs time to ripen. In this case, the mediator should not force the parties to meet.

If one of the parties goes away on a business trip or on a vacation, the negotiations may have to be suspended. The mediator should be sensitive to other events impinging on the family. For example, when children of a divorcing couple are on summer vacation, there may be less pressure on their parents to resolve a custody dispute. Of course, this problem will have to be settled before the summer is over. A mediator can use such deadlines to encourage the parties to reach agreement.

When should a mediator hold separate meetings?

Parties can't agree unless they face each other across the bargaining table, but much of the preliminary work may be done in separate sessions, where positions can be explored and alternatives suggested. The mediator may serve as a broker for such proposals.

Separate sessions may not be appropriate until the parties trust the mediator. Then separate sessions can be helpful, particularly in the event that joint discussions are not proving fruitful. Continuation of joint sessions at such a time may force the parties into fixed positions from which retreat would be difficult.

The mediator may need time to explore specific areas of accommodation. When a party becomes stubborn or inflexible, a mediator may caucus to explain why further concessions will be necessary.

A mediator may shuttle back and forth between the parties, calling them into joint meetings at appropriate times. By talking in confidence with each party, a mediator can gain a better understanding of the couple's positions. Then, by identifying possible trade-offs or mutual concessions, the mediator can help the parties reach an agreement.

How does the mediator create a productive atmosphere?

Parties like to see progress. Early agreements on minor issues may help pave the way for larger concessions. Success breeds success. When things begin to come together, negotiations may gain momentum and become increasingly productive.

A mediator must control the discussions—no easy task in family mediation. The parties have already fought many battles. Domestic squabbling can be habit-forming. Some ventilation of emotions may be inevitable, but the parties should exercise restraint: personal attacks can inhibit progress. The mediator must keep the talks marching toward a successful conclusion. A mediator is a referee, making sure that the parties fight fair.

When should the parties talk to their lawyers?

Sometimes negotiations on a particular issue can't go forward without additional information. A mediator should encourage the parties to discuss the problem with their own lawyers and to report back. Meanwhile, the negotiations can focus on other issues.

Most experienced family mediators stay in touch with the couple's attorneys, advising them of progress in the case. A good defense against malpractice is to encourage clients to seek advice from their own lawyers and be certain that the attorneys understand what the mediator is trying to do and approve of these efforts. Don't try to take away the lawyers' clients. Don't put yourself in competition with the attorneys.

How should meetings be structured?

The mediator should arrange the issues in a logical sequence. After becoming acquainted with the case and eliciting confidential information about the parties' priorities, the mediator should devise an appropriate sequence. Some mediators begin with less controversial issues. Others believe in starting with the most crucial issue. This decision will turn on the mediator's sense of strategy. How to best initiate movement toward a successful conclusion? The parties will expect the mediator to fix the order in which issues are discussed. They are relying upon the mediator's experience. It is up to the mediator to schedule the meetings and decide what will be discussed at each session.

How does the mediator facilitate a settlement?

The mediator must help the parties talk about the *right* things in the *right* way. In order to reach a settlement, they will have to make concessions and exchange promises. Whatever they agree upon must be able to survive the stress of future events. By strengthening the parties' ability to transmit information and concessions, the mediator can encourage the negotiating process.

The mediator sets the rules under which the parties communicate: certain kinds of statements are forbidden; others are encouraged. Face-to-face negotiations should be relevant and productive. The mediator may have to persuade the parties to abandon negative habits that they have picked up over the years, such as constantly blaming each other, destroying whatever affection may still exist between them. Maintaining a productive interchange can be difficult. A good mediator learns how to help the parties exchange promises, serving as a bridge between them.

"My role," one mediator explained, "is to convert negative intimacy into something like a business relationship. I try to comb out the irritants that have crept into their relationship. When they talk, they no longer stumble over their feelings. Then they can develop a working arrangement."

The mediator helps to define the issues, clarifying any misconceptions that the parties may have about the nature of their conflict. They shouldn't worry about what other people may think. The mediator must persuade them that their future is more important than saving face. By helping the parties gain such insight, the mediator can guide them away from guilt-ridden, adversarial attitudes. This aspect of the mediator's task can be an uphill battle. Many parties become fascinated with demonstrating each other's guilt and their own innocence. Only after this tactic is laid aside can problem-solving become possible.

What does the mediator do about stress?

A family mediator can refer a client to therapy when that is indicated. The mediator should be aware of the likelihood of stress. If one of the parties is too emotional to negotiate, the mediator should adjourn the sessions until the situation can be repaired. Several well-known mediators are family therapists and may be particularly good with such clients. Nevertheless, the line between mediation and therapy should be clearly drawn. A therapist who has assumed responsibility for a client's mental health should not continue to act as a mediator.

Should a mediator push for quick settlement?

In theory, the mediator encourages the parties to negotiate their own agreement. In practice, a mediator should not let an inexperienced party rush into an improvident settlement.

Some people are particularly vulnerable. They become desperate during divorce negotiations, grabbing the first offer that is made. The level of financial support may be totally inadequate.

In one case, a detective hired by the husband apprehended the wife in bed with her lover. The husband and his father persuaded the woman to sign an agreement giving up custody of the two children, the family home, and the automobile. She was to receive $55 a week for sixteen weeks. A court had no trouble overturning that contract.

Sometimes a husband may agree to pay more than he can afford. Temporary feelings of guilt may overwhelm him. If he becomes unable to meet his obligations, he may default, leaving his former spouse with even less money than she would have obtained from a more moderate settlement.

A mediator should never encourage the parties to conclude a final settlement before they are ready. In *Divorce Mediation: A Practical Guide for Therapists and Counselors* (1982), John Haynes describes such a couple.

Ira and Bev had been married for thirty years. They had four children, aged twenty-eight, twenty-three, sixteen, and eleven. Ira earned a modest salary as an accountant. Bev had never held an outside job. When the couple first came to Haynes, seeking a divorce, he realized that they couldn't sustain themselves on the husband's salary. He suggested that Bev attend a vocational school. She also had to learn to drive. Ira agreed to pay for Bev's driving lessons if she would get a job.

A noticeable change took place in Bev's personality as she began to grow more independent. Even after Ira broke off an affair that he was having with another woman, Bev wanted to leave her husband. She was developing her own life.

Since they could not afford to separate, it was agreed that they would wait until Bev graduated from her book-keeping course. Another issue arose. Bev had been refused a job because she needed a hearing aid. Ira agreed to pay for that, too, as long as Bev continued looking for a job. Finally, she found a job. At that point, Bev agreed to move out of the house. A settlement was reached.

How does the mediator prepare the parties?

When the parties start negotiating, they must be ready to do so. A mediator should stress the importance of preparation. In family mediation, the mediator must help each person prepare.

Preparation involves organization. Both parties must analyze the situation and select a strategy. They will have to justify each demand. Information must be accumulated and prepared for presentation. Each argument has to be considered from the other party's point of view. What will convince the adversary to make a concession? Often in family mediation, the most compelling points are based on the best interests of the children.

A negotiator must know what to ask for and should plan in advance exactly how to make demands. Often, a practice presentation can be made to the mediator, who may suggest ways to strengthen the case.

It is important for both parties to try to anticipate the other's reaction to each demand. Again, the mediator can provide insights.

How should negotiations be conducted?

When both parties are prepared, they are finally ready to present their demands. Then an exchange can take place. The mediator should facilitate this process. Some parties are incapable of discussing certain issues without assistance.

The negotiations should proceed in a logical sequence.

Often, the discussions will be interrupted. Parties may display anger or inject inflammatory rhetoric. These outbursts may block communication. The mediator should prohibit anything that does not contribute to a solution.

Progress toward a settlement requires willingness to compromise. As the parties engage in bargaining, they commit themselves to the success of this process. A settlement becomes their goal.

The mediator must establish a relationship that will increase the parties' motivation to settle. If they fail to reach agreement, the mediator will share in that failure. If they fail to learn from the experience, the mediator is seriously at fault. They should be assured that the mediator is counting on them to succeed.

What are the mechanics of negotiating?

Negotiators attempt to solve problems by exchanging mutual promises and concessions. In family negotiations, the roadblocks to settlement may involve misunderstandings between the parties. When the parties share the facts and talk about their perceptions, the central disputed issue may dissipate. But some issues may have to be resolved through bargaining. A review of this process follows.

• *Bargaining requires understanding.* Individuals bring different values to the bargaining table. First, you must understand your own goals and how important they are to you. Then, you must try to understand your adversary's behavior. How will that person respond? What will motivate those actions? The answers will tell you what arguments and pressures are apt to move the other party.

• *People are motivated by a desire for fulfillment.* The needs and desires of an adversary provide the key to the bargaining process. Each party will want something from the other. The mutual satisfaction of such desires leads to a solution. When the parties understand each other's needs a successful settlement becomes likely.

• *Parties with high aspirations tend to succeed the most.* If you want more, you get more. Negotiators who expect less are usually satisfied with less. Goals are set by each party's aspiration level and by the degree of risk that person is willing to take. People base their demands upon their expectation of success and upon their evaluation of the potential rewards and risks involved.

• *Parties adjust their goals during negotiations.* Negotiators attempt to change their adversary's level of aspiration. Every demand or concession, every new fact or argument, each threat should be calculated to reduce your opponent's expectations. You should try to create doubt in the other party's mind. The object is to achieve the highest level of satisfaction without forcing your opponent into an impasse.

• *The result depends upon relative power.* Power is reflected in ability to influence the behavior of your adversary. Power is relative, and it may be real or apparent. Your power is effective to the extent that it is accepted by your adversary. Influence is a form of power, one that is hard to measure. When preparing for negotiations, you should evaluate the power equation between yourself and your opponent. Think about the power of reward and punishment. Commitment can be a source of power. Parties who are committed to something may have strength or weakness. Consider the power of legitimacy, a mysterious, almost hypnotic influence. People often respect procedures or traditions without questioning their applicability. The law itself has force because of its legitimacy. The reputation of being law-abiding can be a weakness.

• *Knowledge can become a source of power.* The more one knows about the other's needs and objectives, the stronger one may be in negotiations. Not always, though.

A person willing to take risks and to tolerate uncertainties has power. An ignorant person, unaware of the risks, may exert power. In a rational world, the madman may be king. A party constrained by time may give up strength to a more patient negotiator. If you can persuade your adversary to accept a time limit, you may create additional pressure. The ability to plan, to set priorities, to anticipate actions, and to develop a bargaining strategy can lend power to the negotiator. This, too, is a form of knowledge.

• *Persuasion*. Before knowing how to be persuasive, you will have to appraise your adversary's motives and values. A threat may create an atmosphere of hostility. A rejection may be acceptable if based on mutual concerns rather than differences. Arousing a need in the other party and then satisfying that need can be a particularly effective technique of persuasion. There are many such arrows in the professional negotiator's quiver.

• *Confidence*. Negotiators should guard against lowering their own expectations. An advocate should believe that the outcome will be positive. Confidence is crucial.

• *Status*. Status can be important. For example, a wage-earning head of the family has a strong psychological advantage. Status affects the expectations of other members of the family.

These elements of behavior are common to all negotiations: need fulfillment, aspiration level, influence, persuasion, self-confidence, and status. With these mechanical elements in mind, the negotiator can manipulate the bargaining process. What is particularly interesting about family disputes is that while some issues are adversarial and lend themselves to nose-to-nose bargaining, others are saturated with mutual interests. When the husband and wife are picking through the family silver, there may be nothing to do but swap spoons and forks. When they are selecting a summer camp for Junior, they ought to focus on what is best for their child. The mechanics of negotiating that I have just described are applicable to situations in which more for you means less for me. Often in family disputes, that approach is not appropriate. The parties may have to approach their problems in a more positive way. It is up to the mediator to help them make the transition.

A mediator does not simply let things happen but plays an active part in the negotiations, helping the parties achieve a result that will benefit the entire family.

Should a mediator help the parties to negotiate?

In family disputes, an individual may need extra help. It would be improper for such a person to try to bargain without special preparation. This is crucial. A family mediator is obliged to coach a weaker party. No two people have equal bargaining ability. The mediator may help both parties to prepare, but one is likely to require more help.

Sometimes, of course, such inequality is not reparable. Then bargaining may be improper. Not every family dispute should be settled through mediation. Let's face it: some people can't be trusted to handle their own affairs. The only way to protect them is to turn their affairs over to an attorney. Each mediator must determine this question on a case-by-case basis. Even after a settlement has been reached, a mediator may wonder whether the arrangement was fair. Was it an equitable settlement?

The weaker party may go to a lawyer who may decide to try to overturn the agreement in court. What if the judge finds that the plaintiff was incapable of negotiating? The mediator may be sued for participating in a charade. Even if the likelihood of the mediator's being held liable is remote, defending such a lawsuit can be troublesome in itself. In any case, there can be no doubt that a mediator is morally obligated to provide a procedure that is fundamentally fair.

What are some tricks of the trade?

When the parties begin negotiating, the mediator assumes a difficult role, helping them to make concessions. Experienced mediators use a variety of techniques at this point.

• *Opening channels of communication.* Many people have forgotten how to communicate. Children say their parents don't listen. Wives claim that their husbands no longer hear what they say. Older people complain that they have become invisible to their children. Failure to communicate is a common problem.

The mediator must find out whether the parties are getting through to each other. Are they able to discuss the issues? Have they stopped listening? Sometimes they may be totally bored with each other or a particular subject may be too painful to discuss. A skillful mediator may be able to reopen channels of communication that have not been used for years. An experienced mediator explains: "During the initial meeting, I listen very carefully. When I hear something that one of the parties is not responding to, I spell it out. I am constantly digging under the surface, asking questions and explaining. Sometimes even the most obvious points are not being heard. I make certain that they are."

• *Translating for deaf ears.* Members of a family talk, but do not necessarily hear what is being said. The mediator must translate, first identifying whatever is blocking the parties' ability to understand each other. Do the words carry different meanings for each party? Are values in conflict?

"It can be very frustrating," one mediator told me. "They are speaking the same language. They have shared a marriage. Their bodies could communicate. Now they seem totally incapable of exchanging information. Sometimes I suspect that they are communicating in some secret code. I have to make them use a language that all three of us can understand.''

• *Creating doubts*. The mediator must challenge the respective assumptions of the parties. Are their expectations realistic? Can their demands be justified? The mediator has to confront the parties with reality.

When each party must defend its own position, priorities are likely to shift. The mediator forces them to confront the facts, all the while stressing the consequences of failing to resolve the conflict. By creating doubts in the minds of both parties, the mediator persuades them to compromise.

• *Digging for concessions*. The mediator has to try to discover each party's fundamental needs. Various alternatives that a party might never discuss in joint sessions can be considered in private meetings. The mediator may even suggest possible swaps.

The mediator looks for overlapping concessions. Once positions coincide, the mediator tries to narrow the gap, moving toward agreement: "Usually, when I finally bring the parties together, I know that I have a settlement. But I must be sure that they will stick to their part of the deal. Each has agreed to make mutual concessions. I have to facilitate the exchange. That is when mediating becomes dicey.'' This mediator adds that she has various ways of encouraging her clients to close the gap: "Either I can offer the package as my idea, or I can present it as a hypothetical solution. Neither party wants to be the first one to concede. I have to make it look like a simultaneous exchange.''

The mediator constantly looks for trade-offs. If the husband can pay more money per month, the wife will let him have the car. If grandmother can stay at her sister's house until October, her son's family will take her for the rest of the winter. The mediator has to discover areas for compromise. Relying on these, the mediator often can devise the formula for settlement.

"A mediator can be innovative, but only if he or she has taken the trouble to study the case carefully," a mediator told me. He explains that he jots down various alternatives, examining in detail the pros and cons of each arrangement, calculating the costs, and outlining the arguments that would have to be made: "As an attorney, I am a persuasive advocate. When I hit upon an attractive solution, I go all out to sell it to the parties. Usually, I succeed."

• *Keeping discussions alive.* Negotiations can break down because of lack of progress. The mediator must try to persuade the parties to continue working toward a settlement. Momentum is important. A mediator has to use success as an incentive. The parties should leave each session with some understanding of what must be done to achieve some goal at the next session. The mediator may give them homework, ask them to study a particular problem, and tell them to come back ready to discuss the next issue.

In family mediation, the individuals must continue to cope with their troubled lives. The mediator has to link one session with the next. It may be a mistake to allow too much time between sessions. One of the parties may fall under the spell of someone who is working against a settlement. Events that take place outside may prejudice the negotiations.

• *Nailing down concessions.* Sometimes the mediator will discover privately that an exchange is possible, but one party is reluctant to make an offer unless the other party will offer a concession in exchange. Unfortunately, the mediator can't promise that both sides will follow the script. Personal trust between the parties and the mediator becomes essential. Indeed, the entire agreement usually rests upon good faith.

Sometimes mediators get burnt. As one divorce mediator told me:

Once or twice, people have failed to meet their commitments. In one case, the husband walked away from the entire agreement, moving to Mexico with his girlfriend a few months after the final divorce. In another situation, the wife reneged on commitments that she had made in a private session. Now I explain to both parties that their future depends upon their being able to trust each other. When they give me their word on something, I do everything I can to nail it down.

• *Bringing the negotiations to a close.* When one individual is particularly stubborn, the mediator may decide that no settlement is possible. A wife demands to remain in the family house, expecting her husband to pay the expenses. The mediator tells her that it is out of the question. If she refuses to budge, what then? This can provoke a crisis in the negotiations. The mediator may have to exert pressure on both parties to close the gap. The mediator must launch a final assault, warning them that this is the last chance to settle.

The mediator should do whatever must be done to bring the parties together. The closing is the crucial test of the process.

Should a mediator suggest a settlement formula?

During the end game, a mediator will make suggestions, drawing upon experience with earlier cases. Successful proposals for settlement usually come only when the parties have reached the closing stage in their negotiations. The mediator should be sure that the parties welcome such an initiative.

Premature suggestions may upset the strategy of a party who has been waiting patiently for a final concession. A cautious mediator will float ideas privately before introducing them in a joint session. If the move would be untimely, the mediator will delay. If a suggestion is unacceptable to one party, there may be no need to disclose it to the other. If the proposal is acceptable to both, the mediator must decide when and how to inject it into the discussion.

Parties make hard choices as they approach a closing. Are the remaining issues worth an impasse? The mediator may describe the terrible things that will occur if the parties are unable to agree. A mediator has to exert pressure on both parties, pushing them to make final concessions. But the mediator can't press too far. An agreement is worthless if the parties don't honor it.

If the mediator's recommendation is rejected by the parties, the problem becomes more difficult. That is why such suggestions should be made late in the negotiations, when the mediator can forecast the terms of a possible settlement.

When the parties have rejected a number of alternatives, a final recommendation from the mediator may be necessary. Under no circumstances should such a suggestion come as a surprise. A mediator should never submit a settlement proposal at a joint session unless both parties have indicated that they would welcome such an intervention.

The mediator should remind the parties how much time and effort they have invested in attempting to reach a settlement. The mediator should give the parties one last opportunity to compromise in their dispute. Then, if the parties are still unable to agree, they might be asked whether they are willing to authorize the mediator to decide the remaining issues as an arbitrator.

Finally, the ultimate throw of the dice: "As long as you adhere to your present positions, no agreement seems possible and there is no point holding further meetings. In light of this, I shall propose one final formula for compromise." This may involve splitting the difference between their final positions.

Parties will usually settle. More often than not, if they can be persuaded to engage in sustained discussions, they are willing to make mutual concessions that lead to a solu-

tion. Once they become committed to the process of problem-solving, they discover that they want to succeed.

Not everyone is convinced that this is good. To express
the other side, I will quote a law professor:

> This process, which you call divorce mediation, is nothing
> more nor less than manipulation. Your mediator acts as ring-
> master, persuading these unsophisticated couples to jump
> through hoops. You can't pretend that the parties are accom-
> plished negotiators. They canter around the tent for as many
> exercise periods as the mediator wishes to impose upon them
> and then he cracks the whip and they gallop together into an
> agreement. Whatever you say about it, the mediator calls the
> tune.

Of course, I don't agree with this view. A mediator
can't force clients to come to an agreement. They know
that they will have to live under its terms. Mediation can
facilitate the process of settlement but the parties maintain
control. Law professors are a suspicious tribe.

What if a settlement is not possible?

Not every case can be settled. If a mediator decides either
that a settlement is not possible or that a settlement would
be unfair to a party or to the children or other people who
might be prejudiced, the mediator should stop pushing.

A mediator is not responsible for the mischief parties
cook up on their own. Parties are free to negotiate their
own deal. At the outset, it was made clear that the mediator
would not decide for them.

Sometimes, a mediator finds it difficult to let go. A word
of caution from an experienced mediator: "For some mediators, the temptation to play God becomes overwhelming. The clients look to you for help. It is all too easy to
tell them what to do. A mediator should resist that temptation. They should be made responsible for their own actions. It is not up to the mediator to convert bad parents

into something better. Our obligation is, at the most, to give them an informed choice.''

As we have seen, the parties can terminate their discussions at any point. A mediator can also quit. When settlement is impossible or when one of the parties can't be trusted, it is time to bail out.

How is the agreement finalized?

When the parties reach a settlement, the mediator will usually assist them by putting the agreement into writing. It may be enough to scribble some rough notes for them to initial. If the dispute involves a marital separation agreement or a substantial property settlement, a summary of the parties' agreement should be prepared for their lawyers. At that point, the attorneys will have an opportunity to safeguard their clients' legal rights and interests. In any case, the mediator may want to schedule a final session to answer any questions about the agreement. Then the contract can be put in proper form and finalized, legally if necessary. Of course, some agreements do not have to be incorporated in a formal legal document. For example, a settlement between a teenage daughter and her parents about her allowance, the use of the car, how much television she can watch, or when she must get home on week nights can be written down and pinned up on the kitchen wall. A seemingly trivial agreement, but one that may resolve dozens of potential squabbles during the school year.

What does a lawyer do when a mediated agreement is submitted for review?

An attorney who is asked to review a mediated agreement sometimes faces difficult choices. Should the attorney simply read the agreement and comment on its legal aspects? Should the anatomy of the negotiations be analyzed? Should the lawyer investigate the facts? What if the attorney thinks that the deal was bad? Should the client be told to break it?

A lawyer will want to ascertain whether the client is happy with the agreement. Is it totally understood? It may be helpful to ask the client's perception of the various provisions.

After an explanation of some of the legal implications, the client may say that the mediator gave a different impression. What then? What if the agreement is ambiguous? Should the attorney discuss the document with the mediator? Should the mediator's explanation be accepted?

Obviously, the reviewing lawyer may have some concerns. On the other hand, it may not be helpful to upset the deal. It is probably best to talk it out with the client.

When is the mediation over?

When the parties have completed their negotiations, the mediator is no longer needed. Whether the dispute involved a teenage boy who negotiated his way out from under a domineering mother or a couple who went through the throes of an angry divorce, the final agreement completes the task. The parties need have nothing further to do with the mediator. Now it is up to them to live under the agreement they have constructed.

Should a mediator have power to arbitrate?

In *Structured Mediation in Divorce Settlements* (1979), the late O. J. Coogler defined mediation in simple terms: "When two or more persons are having trouble resolving a controversy, they may agree to turn to a neutral third person who will help them resolve it. Agreeing to work out their problems in this way is called mediation " (p. 2).

Coogler explained that it is the responsibility of the parties to agree on the issues. Other than establishing that all relevant information has been collected and examined by the parties, a mediator need only determine that the agreement is within socially accepted guidelines. The Coogler version of mediation is called "structured mediation."

Coogler was trained as an attorney. Following his own divorce and some exposure to Transactional Analysis, Coogler became convinced that there had to be a better way than the adversary system for people to negotiate a marital dissolution: "I am indebted to my former wife and the two attorneys who represented us in our divorce for making me aware of the critical need for a more rational, more civilized way of arranging a parting of the ways. Her life, my life, and our children's lives were unnecessarily embittered by that experience" (p. v).

Structured mediation was developed by Coogler in the mid-1970s. Using a foundation grant, he trained hundreds of divorce mediators. He founded the Family Mediation Association.

The system is called structured because it follows fixed procedures. Coogler saw a family as a partnership. When it comes time to dissolve a marriage, the wife's dependent relationship has to be terminated. Both parents have to continue to care for the children. Coogler viewed mediation as a way to move from the partnership of marriage to the partnership of single parenthood. Coogler called structured mediation "a new kind of mediation." It was created as a self-contained system. Issues are defined, and the various options are systematically examined in the light of their probable consequences. The procedure was described in detail in his pioneering book.

If the parties cannot agree, the issues are decided by arbitration. Coogler drew liberally from the Commercial Arbitration Rules of the American Arbitration Association (AAA) for his Marital Arbitration Rules. In fact, he simply inserted FMA wherever the AAA appeared in the Rules.

Incorporating arbitration into the structured mediation process, in Coogler's words, "avoids the use of impasse as a bargaining strategy.'' That detracts from the voluntary nature of family mediation. In my opinion, families should not be forced to arbitrate. They should be allowed to terminate their negotiations at any time. No one should be tied to a particular mediator or to a particular agency.

I am convinced that negotiated settlements are a preferable way to resolve most family disputes. Competent mediators should be able to persuade their clients to continue in mediation until a settlement is achieved. Any requirement that the couple agree in advance to submit unresolved issues to arbitration injects an unnecessary compulsion into the mediation process. Most family mediation centers do not advocate mandatory arbitration. Their procedures are truly voluntary. The Family Mediation Rules of the American Arbitration Association reflect that same attitude.

When the parties have reached agreement, it is appropriate for them to agree to arbitrate any disputes that they may have in the future. This is a good way to avoid having to go back to court. But arbitration should not be a required part of the mediation process.

Conclusion

This chapter describes the nuts and bolts of the family mediation process and how it encourages interpersonal negotiations. The mediator's function is described in some detail. A step-by-step description is included so that the reader will gain an understanding of how a mediator is likely to proceed with the task of bringing the parties together. The mechanics of the negotiating process are covered, as are the practical techniques of the mediator. Finally, the role of the attorney is outlined.

3

Divorce Mediation: A New Profession

AFTER WORLD WAR II, millions of marriages came un-
glued. Divorces had been running at about two per thousand: the postwar period saw this rate more than double.
In the 1960s and seventies, again the rate more than doubled. By then, eight million households were headed by
single women.

Forty percent of all American marriages are likely to
end in divorce. Divorce involves over a million children
each year. No small problem.

During recent years, the rate of increase has tapered
off. What about the future? The stability of marriage is
closely related to employment. If the 1980s is marked by
high unemployment, divorce may increase. Indeed, couples may never marry. Even now, in low-income groups,
marriage is not all that fashionable.

More women are working today than ever before. They
express their independence by staying single or by getting

divorced. There are twice as many unmarried women between twenty-five and twenty-nine as there were ten years
ago. For a working woman, marriage is not always a good
deal since it may mean that she has to cover two functions:
"While a woman may be striving very hard to advance her
career and contribute to the family till, her time is also
largely occupied with shopping, cleaning house, and preparing dinner for her husband," noted Dr. Selma Miller in
the June 1982 *Harper's Bazaar*.

No wonder many "superwomen" discover that being
single offers the more rewarding lifestyle. The romantic
expectations of young, two-career lovebirds fray at the
edges, particularly in cities, where community pressures
don't encourage couples to stay married.

According to Dr. Laura Singer, president of Save a
Marriage, an organization based in New York City,
"We're living in a culture of instant gratification. If things
do not work out, there's a feeling of being able to leave and
find something better." If marriage turns out to be a boring
extra job, it makes sense for the career woman to concentrate on her "real" job, the one she gets paid for.

Incompatibility is the most common reason given for
divorce. At one time, it was the husband who found his
wife uninteresting. Recently, women have been initiating a
higher percentage of splits. "I just came to the conclusion
that I was missing something by being married. Life was
passing me by. There are so many things that I want to do,
want to be free to do for myself," one woman explained.
She negotiated a divorce that financed her acquisition
of an MBA, leading to an executive job in international
banking.

Our attitude toward marriage is changing rapidly. Not
everyone's of course. Adult values are the result of two
cultures, that of our childhood, when marriage was based
upon male dominance, and that of our maturity, when
equality became the rage. The rules of the game have been
rewritten during our lives. The game goes on: marriage
may still involve romance, but couples have to cope with

earning a living, raising a family, and overcoming health problems. And modern marriage can be tough. It demands more of both adults and children, who today are expected to participate in the family on more or less equal terms. Children have the additional task of bringing their parents up to date. If an adult has been left behind by the times, someone must speak up. Often, that someone is a child.

What is divorce?

State government requires that family courts be involved in the ending of a marriage. The procedure varies from state to state. Nor is it always easy to determine which state has jurisdiction over a divorce.

In order to terminate a marriage, the parties must obtain a divorce decree. Before granting a divorce, the courts will look into child custody and the financial arrangements for the family. The decree will determine the best interests of any children and may require that marital property be divided according to local law.

The court's authority to allocate marital resources and to order support payments forms the background against which negotiations can take place. Often a husband will be attempting to minimize his obligations, retaining as much property and income as he can for his new life. The wife, in turn, will be making demands for her own support. The wife may also speak for the children. The interests of the children may or may not be protected or represented by attorneys.

In some cases, other family interests will be involved in a divorce. The failure of a marriage involves more than two people. Behind the principals, a host of interests and influences will appear, including other individuals. Divorce requires the reordering of manifold relationships among the various relatives and friends who have participated in the relationship. The husband and wife may cut away certain intimate parts of their relationship, but many other strands remain, binding them to their children and others with whom they will continue to relate.

A recent case from San Diego illustrates the process of mediation in a divorce case. The parties had been trying for over a year to untangle their marriage. The case was referred to the Divorce and Child Custody Mediation Service of San Diego by the wife's attorney, who had heard about the service and thought that the couple were good candidates for mediation.

The couple had been married six years, were in their thirties, attractive, articulate, and well educated. They had a four-year-old son. The husband held a management position with a large company. The wife was working part-time. They owned their home, some other rental property, two cars, stocks, and personal property. The wife had filed for divorce almost a year before coming to mediation. The court ordered the couple to continue living in the same house. Living together was becoming increasingly difficult.

The issues between them included all the typical aspects of a divorce. Dr. Faye J. Girsh accepted the case for mediation. In a letter to me, she described her technique:

> The method of mediation I use is to meet with the couple with my attorney-consultant present during all of the sessions. During the initial meeting we explain the mediation process, determine the issues that have to be mediated, and the amount of emotional interference that will get in the way. This enables us to screen the candidates and determine how long we think it will take and how much it will cost. We do not accept couples who are extremely angry at each other, who don't trust each other, who have very complex estates, or where one party does not want to be in mediation. During the first meeting we ask the couple to prepare statements of their assets and their monthly financial needs. The sessions are one hour in length, unless a longer session is warranted.
>
> My role as a psychologist is to make sure that both parties are heard and understood and to sort out and deal with any emotional issues. The attorney provides advice based on what the courts might do. He also tells them about the tax consequences.

Courtland Palmer, an attorney who works with Dr. Girsh, favors mediation because "when you talk something out, you feel better about the results. You stick with the agreement because you don't feel it was a compromise forced on you by someone who had better legal advice." During the first session, the couple were asked to sign a waiver that the attorney-consultant did not represent either party and that they agreed to the mediation process.

In a series of eight sessions, held over a period of six months, all of the issues were resolved. The most important problem was to reach agreement about custody and about the house, so that the couple could live apart and reduce tension. They were delighted to learn about joint custody and decided that the wife would stay in the house. The husband would move out. The child would stay with the mother Thursday through Monday morning and with the father the rest of the week. After they settled that question, they negotiated the support issues. No child support was to be paid by either party. The husband agreed to pay spousal support in diminishing amounts for a fixed period of time until the wife could earn enough to provide for her own needs. The sharing of marital assets was also worked out. The agreement was taken to the couple's attorneys and approved.

The cost of this mediation was $1,000. The couple had already paid several thousand dollars in lawyers' fees before coming to mediation. They paid an additional $200 for an attorney's services after the mediation. Palmer says that trying the case in court would have cost at least ten times that much.

Why is divorce litigation so bitter?

Some lawyers take advantage of the situation. By advising their clients to go to war, they inflame their confrontation. When a lawyer is told to do "everything necessary to win," a lawsuit may be inevitable. No wonder that some divorce lawyers are called "bombers."

Take a typical couple, married a dozen years, with a child or two. They are living together in a suburban house. The husband is working. They are reasonable and responsible people, not really mad at each other but no longer in love. They want a divorce. Each one goes to an attorney. What happens next?

The wife's lawyer advises her to take the money out of the couple's joint bank account. The husband's lawyer tells him to cancel his wife's charge accounts. And then? The husband goes to the bank for some cash. No money. He is furious. Down the street his wife goes to the market to buy the childrens' dinner. No credit. She is humiliated. Both have been warned to leave the talking to their lawyers. Can you imagine how much anger such tactics generate? Remember, the lawyers are duty-bound to protect the legal interests of their clients. They are captives of the adversary process. The system is at fault.

Historically, divorce litigation was based upon fault, reflecting a desire to punish couples who contemplated divorce. Unfortunately, the bricks often fell on the children. Contested divorce cases could devastate a family, tearing apart everyone involved at exactly the time when they required help to rebuild their lives.

Family lawyers find it difficult to be supportive during a client's divorce. Until recently, attorneys had no choice but to take sides. Now, in some jurisdictions, attorneys are permitted to mediate. They take the bitterness out of divorce cases. Some lawyers are not comfortable with this approach. Others welcome mediation as an opportunity to help their clients.

Divorce litigation is big business, particularly when wealthy clients are involved. Over a million divorce cases each year! Think of it! New York family law specialist Doris Freed claims that "more than 50 percent of all civil cases filed are in the family court system. In some states, this represents as much as two-thirds of the civil case-load.''

No-fault divorce was expected to reduce the volume of divorce litigation, but some recent statutory changes have made it difficult to settle divorce cases under this system. By eliminating the ''mother's preference'' in custody cases and by requiring courts to determine the ''best interests of the child'' and by establishing the doctrine of ''equitable distribution'' for marital property, state legislatures may be encouraging even more litigation. These three changes in family law have complicated divorce cases: discovery procedures have become more extensive, and now trials have to cover more material. Whenever parties are forced to resolve their problems in court, bitterness floods back into their relationship.

What is the role of the divorce lawyer?

As we have seen, the divorce lawyer is expected to grab everything possible for the client. That is a tough adversary role. A lawyer's reputation is built on a record of success, measured by the number of victories.

A few divorce lawyers engage in questionable activities. In one recent case private detectives had been retained to help a wife get back her jewelry from her prior residence. The detectives threw the husband against a wall; the couple's two children watched in horror. The wife's attorney was sued by the husband for assault and battery. The jury awarded a substantial verdict against the attorney. Divorce lawyers are expected to be aggressive. Often, that is what they are hired for. But when they go too far in supporting the desires of their client, they may subject themselves to liability.

In court, the lawyer speaks for the client. The children may not be represented by an attorney. The lawyers for both parties are expected to speak for the best interests of the child. Since they are on opposite sides of the case, their views are likely to clash. Then, the judge may turn to an outside expert for guidance.

It is interesting that the needs of the parents are seldom referred to by a court even though their interests are also at stake. The court's avowed concentration upon the child's so-called best interests sometimes smacks of hypocrisy. Recent surveys indicate that many couples are unhappy about how their separation was handled in family court. The trend toward mediation flows from such discontent. Parties can avoid having a judge decide by resolving their problems privately.

Does mediation encourage divorce?

A divorce mediator should determine whether the marriage is dead. When not convinced that a separation is inevitable, mediators will try to bring about a reconciliation. If the husband and wife are willing to work on their relationship, that may be possible. A trial separation may help some couples appreciate what they once valued in their marriage.

A case sent to me by mediator Phoebe Prosky provides an illustration. A couple was referred to her by a mutual friend. The wife, who was of European origin, had been married before and had a twenty-one-year-old son. She taught at an eastern university. The husband owned a business in mail order books.

The wife wanted a separation because she wanted to return to her native country, where she felt her academic opportunities would be greater. Also, she had become involved with a man in her native country and wanted to pursue that relationship. She no longer loved her husband.

The husband did not want a divorce. He thought that their problems could be resolved and wanted to maintain his relationship with their two young sons.

When the couple came to Dr. Prosky's office, they were on the verge of a lawsuit. At first, Prosky supported the husband's efforts to save the marriage. She suggested that they attempt to mediate their problems, refraining from litigation during a period of exploration. Still, the wife could not be persuaded. She was so stubborn that a court custody battle seemed inevitable. Both parents wanted the children to live with them. Prosky persuaded the couple not to go to court. A lawsuit would intensify the anger and mistrust between them and jeopardize the familial relationships that they would share in the future. They agreed because of their concern for the children.

In Prosky's words:

> My work then involved placing responsibility for the situation as strongly and clearly at the doorstep of each as possible, eliciting the needs and wishes of each for the next period in their lives and helping to construct a life form based on the determination of responsibility and need. In this way, we dealt with the children's living arrangements, property issues and the particulars of the shape of their ongoing family life.

An arrangement was worked out. The children would travel with their mother to Europe for the summer. At the end of that time, the husband would be visiting Europe on a business trip. He would take the children on a vacation. Then the husband and children would return to the United States for the winter. The wife would remain in Europe, with a few trips to the United States during the course of the year. This plan was presented to the children as the way in which family life would proceed in the coming year.

A financial arrangement was also agreed upon. The couple were able to divide their possessions. As the mediator pointed out, "All of this required a tremendous amount of forbearance and the suspension of mistrust—a difficult operation at such a critical moment. Yet they managed it as a family and are now in the middle of the first year of their arrangement. They agreed to plan each period of their lives as seemed best at the time for themselves and the children." The couple finally obtained a divorce, but Prosky had done her best to keep them together.

In those kinds of situations, a mediator may try to stabilize a family. The couple's quarrels may be driving them apart. By helping them to communicate, a mediator may save their marriage. Several studies have demonstrated that mediation can improve relationships between marriage partners who were previously hostile. The court process is likely to worsen family relationships by feeding on the anger generated in a deteriorating marriage.

Is divorce mediation always helpful?

According to John Haynes, a mediator from Long Island: "Mediation won't work for those couples who are out to kill each other, but it's ideal for those who need a nonadversarial process. . . . I see mediation becoming the first choice for one-third of the couples seeking to settle a divorce dispute."

Some couples can agree amicably. Others are so hungry for revenge that they can't resist the lure of the courts. If parties are unwilling to negotiate or are so mad that it is impossible for them to communicate except through attorneys, mediation may be out of the question. Litigation does provide an opportunity to punish an opponent, but at great emotional and financial cost to both parties.

Mediation meets the needs of people who are able to talk but need professional help in finding a solution. The parties must be willing to compromise. Most people know what is best for them. Given a fair opportunity, they can solve their own problems. Of course, there are people who seem to have an insatiable appetite for fighting. "I am not worried about mediation taking away my practice," one divorce lawyer told me. "In my community, there are plenty of people who like to fight. When they get bored with their house and their cars and their marriage, I am there to give them a new outlet for their aggression.''

Even when the mediation does not result in a settlement, the process has not necessarily been a failure. Sometimes the parties have gained valuable insights from their attempt to settle.

The Minnesota Mediation & Counseling Center was approached by two attorneys who represented a husband and wife in a divorce action that had been going on nearly nine months. The attorneys had expected the clients to settle, but the settlement fell through. All of the preparation for a trial had been completed and a trial date set. The attorneys were convinced that a trial would only make things worse. Anyway, their clients were running out of patience. The attorneys were encouraging their clients to mediate. They would put off the trial pending mediation.

The couple had been married for twenty years but had been separated for almost a year before mediation began. They had three children, aged fourteen, eleven, and nine. Both parties were employed. The husband made $40,000 per year as a sales manager. The wife made $10,000 as a secretary. They had not spoken to each other for over nine months. All communication was through their attorneys. The parties themselves were pessimistic about reaching agreement, but they were also sick of fighting.

Property included a house, some savings, a few stocks and bonds, life insurance, cars, household furnishings, and other personal property. Liabilities amounted to about $50,000, mostly the mortgage on the house.

When the mediators met with the couple, both parties seemed tense. The mediators explained the mediation process and its rules. It was decided to use co-mediators, male and female, because of the complexity of the case. The mediators also felt more comfortable working as a team. One had more experience with custody; the other, with property and finances.

The first session took two hours. Both individuals persisted in taking shots at each other. The mediators finally gained control and persuaded them to define the issues and state where they stood on each. Control was achieved by interrupting the parties and reminding them of the rules.

The parties had been asked to bring a list of their demands and to prepare budget and financial sheets. The husband had prepared his material in advance. The wife completed hers in the reception area. The mediators worked from this material during the session. The wife wanted sole custody of the children; the husband could visit them every other weekend and keep them for a month during the summer. The husband wavered between wanting sole and joint custody. The primary disagreement over the house was when it should be sold and how the proceeds should be distributed. Several items of personal property were also at issue, as well as how the outstanding debts should be paid.

The wife requested $900 per month for child support, $300 per month for maintenance, with 40 percent of any salary increases to cover inflation, and half of her attorney fees. The husband was willing to pay $600 for child support and $150 for spousal maintenance. The wife made several unusual demands: the husband would lose visitation rights if he lived with another woman; moreover, he could not open his own business, move out of state, or spend over $100 without her permission. He also had to accept counseling to learn how to deal with the children. These were red flags.

Usually mediation moves from the least difficult to the most difficult matter in order to achieve success early in the process. But here the clients wanted to discuss the custody issue because it was the most pressing. The mediators agreed to take up custody at the next session. Prior to that meeting, the husband's attorney warned the mediators that the husband was reluctant to subject himself to further verbal abuse from his wife. The mediators assured him that either the next session would be more productive or an impasse would be declared. Both attorneys continued to support the mediation process, encouraging their clients to bargain in good faith.

The couple seemed more agreeable during the second session. The wife began by stating that the first session had been extremely helpful to her. She had not been able to express her anger directly to her husband for several months. Both parties stated that they were ready to negotiate. They spent the next two hours discussing custody and were able to reach substantial agreement. They worked out an arrangement but could not decide what to call it. The mediators suggested the term "shared custody."

A third session was scheduled two weeks later, to give the parties time to prepare additional financial sheets. When they arrived, both once again stated that mediation had improved their relationship in that they had become more cooperative about the children and more considerate of each other. Property was discussed next. They reached agreement on allocating personal property. They then tried to negotiate about the house but were unable to agree whether the house should be sold or how to divide the proceeds. The mediators suggested that they discuss support and maintenance, returning to the house later. The budget sheets were also reviewed. Here the couple seemed stubborn, reluctant to depart from their original positions. As tension began to mount, the mediators told them to go home and draft a new proposal.

Each mediator met separately with one of the parties at the beginning of the next session. It was hoped that this might encourage them to be more honest about their intentions. The mediators also wanted to point out some of their less constructive behavior. The female mediator met with the husband. The male mediator met with the wife.

The husband was willing to have a frank discussion about his situation and seemed willing to make certain important concessions. The mediator thought that he was ready to settle on the basis of a reasonable compromise. He had prepared a new settlement offer.

The wife, on the other hand, no longer seemed committed to a settlement. She had put down nothing in writing. She made various allegations about her husband's behavior but refused to accept responsibility for her own actions. The mediator could only encourage her to continue to negotiate but did not feel optimistic.

When the couple was brought together, the wife demanded a copy of her husband's new proposal. He refused to give it to her until she provided one of her own. She became angry and stormed out of the session, yelling obscenities and threats. The mediators did not call her back. And, on that note, the mediation attempt concluded, as a failure.

The mediators prepared a memorandum describing both the tentative agreements that had been reached by the parties. It was hoped that the attorneys might still force a settlement if they knew what had been discussed and could advise their clients accordingly. And, indeed, the couple finally did settle, six days prior to trial. The agreements reached in mediation had shaped their settlement, and they made other concessions under pressure from their attorneys. The attorneys said that the mediation had been helpful. It had provided an opportunity for catharsis.

This mediation took eight hours. The mediators spent an additional three hours drafting documents and conferring with the attorneys and with each other. The total cost to the parties was $600. Even though no settlement was reached, Karen Irvin of the Minnesota Mediation & Counseling Center thinks that this mediation was a partial success.

What does a divorce mediator do?

When couples want a divorce but don't want to go to war against each other in court, and retain a mediator, they may not know exactly what to expect. Sometimes they expect a miracle. The mediator should explain the problems that lie ahead. Something like this: "You want a divorce because you are sick of fighting. You want out. But you should realize that your primary task is to develop a working relationship for the future. In mediation, I will try to teach you to trust each other and to deal constructively about your future plans."

The couple needs a healthy dose of reality. The wife may expect her life to continue much as before. The husband may anticipate a titillating, rejuvenated lifestyle. In fact, the outlook for most divorced couples is forbidding. Money will be tight. Parental responsibilities will continue. The mediator must warn the parties that hard times lie ahead.

When the parties are ready to negotiate, the mediator goes to work. Mediation procedures are informal. The Family Mediation Rules of the American Arbitration Association, which appear in Appendix A, provide a helpful guide.

Adriane Berg, in her course on divorce mediation at the New School in New York City, calls mediation "a revolutionary means of separating, without lengthy litigation or adversarial litigation." She supports the concept because she knows from professional experience how devastating divorce litigation can be upon the members of a family.

What is there about the work of a divorce mediator that is unique? Are there various mediation techniques? Will one mediator's system differ from another's?

Divorce mediators use somewhat different techniques. Isolina Ricci of Palo Alto, California, likes to concentrate upon child custody. Her central concern is with the arrangements for the children after the parents no longer live together. In the rare case in which she mediates property issues, she works with the lawyers.

Ricci is a licensed family therapist, the originator of the two-home approach to joint custody. She has developed a concept of "confluent mediation," which combines mediation with parent training and counseling. Here is a typical case, using her technique.

The Johnsons were referred to Ricci by their attorneys when negotiations broke down over the issue of custody. The marriage had lasted eleven years. Now they were living apart. There were two children, Ann (four) and Bruce (six). The father wanted joint custody, equal time with the children. The mother refused to discuss joint custody. She would not even talk about overnight visitation because the father was involved with another woman.

On the telephone, the mediator learned that the mother was concerned about increasing household costs. The father did not trust a female mediator. He was downright hostile. Ricci mailed copies of her brochure, "Mediation: How It Works in Our Office," and other informative materials. She then scheduled an introductory session. This was followed by separate meetings with the father and the mother. Certain guidelines were accepted at the outset. The parties agreed to leave the children out of the mediation at first but to think about permitting a home visit by the mediator to observe the children in their own environment. The parents ultimately agreed to a minimum of four meetings, with two home visits. No relatives or third persons would participate in the sessions. Both parties agreed to negotiate in good faith. They would share the fees thirty–seventy.

By the end of the first session, the mediator was beginning to understand the problem. A successful outcome seemed possible, but she recommended confluent mediation. The counseling would help the couple's interaction. Postdivorce parent education also would be beneficial.

The Johnsons were at different stages in their emotional development. They also had unequal bargaining skills. Mediation sessions would be interspersed with readings and independent study that would encourage them to accept their separation and prepare them to resolve the question of custody in a realistic way. During the following weeks, the mediator visited them at home; next there was a one-hour joint meeting. Ricci continued to assign homework. The parties were asked to describe their areas of agreement and to develop their ideas for a reasonable settlement.

A temporary arrangement was implemented for a trial period. The parties were asked to keep records on how the plan succeeded. During this period, the parties met several times with the mediator, attempting to design a permanent custody agreement.

The final meetings were spaced several weeks apart. After a total of seven sessions, the parties agreed to a shared custody arrangement. The children would stay 70 percent of the time with their mother, 30 percent with their father. The father agreed to pay family support, based upon the couple's respective incomes and the children's needs. The parents' new relationship was off to a good beginning. The total cost of the mediation was $770.

Other divorce mediators concentrate on property and support. Patrick Westerkamp is a lawyer with experience in labor and commercial arbitration. His approach provides a contrast to Ricci's. Rather than concentrating upon custody and parenting, he tends to focus upon the parties' financial problems.

After eleven years, Ron and Wendy Burton decided to separate. Throughout their marriage, they had been at odds over finances. Each had different aspirations. After every squabble over a purchase, one would give in to the other. As a result, the Burtons lived beyond their means, buying many things on credit. When they came to Westerkamp for mediation, their monthly aftertax income was $2,500. Monthly fixed expenses were $1,446 (mortgage and taxes, $916; car payments, $160; credit card payments, $370). Not much left over. The Burtons had almost no cash reserve.

The negotiations focused on money. The parties agreed that Wendy would have custody of the children. She wanted monthly maintenance payments of $1,250. Ron said that he could afford no more than $200. During the first session, Westerkamp asked the Burtons to prepare separate budgets. These were reviewed at the second meeting. Afterward, the parties agreed to modify their positions.

A successful resolution became possible once the Burtons understood that their home was their only asset. Both wanted the children to live in a suburban environment but their house was too expensive. An apartment would be practical. The Burtons agreed to sell the house to pay their debts and to invest the balance. The income would be used in part to rent an apartment. Additionally, Ron would pay $700 per month for child support and alimony.

The solution to the Burtons' problem turned on facing economic reality. During mediation, the parties saw their house in a new light, no longer the vine-covered cottage of their dreams. The Burtons, through mediation, devised a practical formula for their divorce. Westerkamp saw his role as helping the Burtons to understand the financial problems involved in their separation.

Should a divorce mediator give legal advice?

The mediator's job is to help the parties reach an agreement. A mediator should not provide legal advice. A party who needs such help should be encouraged to consult an attorney. A mediator who is a lawyer may be tempted to give legal opinions. That can be risky because it may subject the mediator to legal liability. A mediator may help to put the parties' agreement in writing, but then it should be submitted to the parties' lawyers.

As I noted earlier, some mediation schemes restrict the parties' right to select a personal attorney. For example, the Family Mediation Association appoints a lawyer for the couple. This system is subject to criticism: clients have the right to retain their own lawyers.

How does divorce affect children?

Conventional wisdom is that divorce tends to stunt a child's development. The child may feel rejected. This seems logical. But some recent studies indicate that such a child is not always handicapped. In fact, a bad marriage may cause more damage. Couples usually divorce for a good reason. One result may be a relieved and happier family, with obvious benefits for the child. Children raised in two-parent homes are not necessarily superior to those raised by a single parent, either in school performance or in social attitudes.

If a child understands the unhappiness of the prior marriage, divorce even may be welcome. When divorce takes a child by surprise, however, damage may occur. A good analysis appears in *Surviving the Breakup,* by Judith S. Wallerstein and Joan Berlin Kelly (1980):

> When the divorce is undertaken thoughtfully by parents who have carefully considered alternatives; when the parents have recognized the expectable psychological, social, and economic consequences for themselves and the children; when they have taken reasonable measures to provide comfort and appropriate understanding to the children; where they have made arrangements to maintain good parent-child relationships with both parents—then those children are not likely to suffer developmental interference or enduring psychological distress as a consequence of the divorce. (p. 316)

Now for the darker side:

> If the divorce is undertaken primarily as a unilateral decision which humiliates, angers, or grieves the other partner; and if the divorce fails to bring relief from marital stress; and if the children are poorly supported and poorly informed or co-opted as allies or fought over in the continuing battle; and if the child feels rejected . . . then the most likely outcome for the children is developmental interference and depression. (pp. 316–317)

Do children usually favor a divorce?

Just because parents decide that their relationship is impossible does not mean that their children necessarily agree. Even a bad marriage may seem acceptable to children.

Younger children often regard divorce as something inflicted upon the family by a "bad" parent. It is pathetically easy to enlist a child in parental conflict. The fault theory may provide the child with a cop-out. If an adult can be blamed, the child does not have to assume responsibility for the divorce. "Daddy left because he didn't love me" translates into "Daddy left because I'm not lovable. No one can love me. I can't even love myself." It may be far better for the child to blame someone else.

Children are seldom asked whether they favor a divorce. When they are asked, the question may be raised in an effort to test their loyalty to one of the parents. They should not be used as pawns in the battle between their parents.

Which parent should get the child?

The question implies that parents own their children. It is more thoughtful to ask which parent should be responsible for the day-to-day care of the child. In many separations, the custody of a child becomes a contest between the parents. The child is looked upon as a prize, something to be fought over. The parents are really fighting over which of them is the better parent, a no-win contest.

Some mediators ask the parents why they want the child. What arrangements will they provide for the child? Why won't they share custody with the other partner? Using such information, the mediator can encourage a formula based upon the best interests of the child. However, the mediator should not make this decision. It is for the parents to make—but not on the basis of a power struggle. The parents should be encouraged to form a "parenting partnership." The mediator should convince them to ask not which parent should "get" the child but how to ensure that the child will "have" both parents. Can a healthy relationship be maintained with both parents?

What is the best custody arrangement?

At one time, the law gave the father an absolute right over his children. Divorce was rare. When it occurred, the father got the kids. Later courts concluded that it was better to give the mother an automatic preference, particularly when the children were young. This doctrine became well established. A father seeking custody had to prove that the mother was incapable of caring for the child.

In recent years, courts seem willing to experiment with schemes for sharing parental responsibility. Usually judges will accept a reasonable arrangement between the parents.

What actually happens may turn on money. Many fathers refuse to provide child support. It is not easy to enforce that obligation. Sometimes support payments are barely adequate. The problem of support is chronic among low-income families. One out of every five children under eighteen lives with a single parent, usually the mother. Many of these women are poor, often surviving on public assistance.

Divorce always stretches a family's budget. This can create hardship. One study has indicated that children living with a single parent are more likely than children from two-parent homes to have a job. Often, they have to work. In some cases, a job may increase their self-reliance. Divorce does not necessarily harm children. Poverty does.

In her upbeat book on joint custody, *Mom's House/ Dad's House,* Ricci (1980) emphasizes the importance of providing a continuing relationship between a child and both parents. She contends that the usual divorce decree, awarding custody to one parent and visitation rights to the other, is harmful. The mother "wins" the case but must assume full responsibility for bringing up the children. The father "loses" the case but must provide financial support even though his children have been taken from him. The child has lost a father. Ricci says that sole custody generates distrust and acrimony between the parents. Certainly, the father is likely to resent the position in which he is placed. Kids also understand the problem: "Daddy sold me to mommy for $200 a month. Mom won the car, the house, and me." Ricci encourages parents to use positive words. Instead of talking about "broken" homes, "victims" of divorce, "winning" in court, or "losing" custody, they should think in terms of "ending" the marriage, "having" two families, and "living" with each parent. The power of semantics!

Not every couple can afford joint custody. Parents in upper-class suburbs may be able to provide double living quarters for their children. For most parents, however, it is a struggle to maintain even one decent place for a child to live. Nevertheless, joint custody is an appealing idea. And there are endless variations on the theme:

- One home during school; the other for weekends and vacations.

- One month in one home; one month in the other.

- Alternating years.

- Child stays in one home; parents switch residences.

- An open schedule to be negotiated by parents and child.

In the negotiations leading to such an arrangement, Ricci stresses the following points:

- The parents are divorcing each other, not their children.

- Each parent accepts parental responsibility.

- Each parent agrees not to interfere with the other parent's approach to childrearing.

- Each parent creates an appropriate home for the children.

Under joint custody, each parent maintains a home and a family relationship with the child. Each child has two homes, two parents.

Some parents are incapable of the selfless love for their children that joint custody requires. Joint custody may encourage other couples to fight over decision after decision as the years roll by.

Ricci carefully explains how couples can readjust their thinking to accommodate joint custody. *Mom's House/ Dad's House* is filled with good advice for well-intentioned parents. It tells how people can be uncoupled from intimacy while continuing their parenting. The book encourages parents to create a working postdivorce relationship.

How should custody disputes be mediated?

Parents feel guilty about breaking up their marriage. They think that custody will demonstrate their love for the children. A mediator can explain that parents don't have to be adversaries on this issue. Their goal should be to work out a sensible arrangement for meeting the needs of the child.

Ricci warns, however, that mediators must be carefully selected: "Many professionals are sympathetic to the idea of removing domestic issues from the combat zone to a neutral ground," but the mediator's philosophy should be similar to that of the parents.

Mediator Ann L. Milne of Madison, Wisconsin, has written extensively on the subject of settling custody disputes (Milne, 1978). Her technique is called "family self-determination." The neutral person is called a "counselor," but the process is mediation. The parents must agree to participate. A series of appointments is arranged and a target date set for reaching agreement. In the counseling sessions, the parties discuss their mutual problems, attempting "to re-create the positive aspects of their relationship." Each parent is asked to suggest an optimum plan for the child's life. What is best for the child? What is best for the parents? The counselor tries to find out what the child wants to have happen. Finally, the counselor attempts to bring the process to a conclusion. After an agreement is reached, the counselor provides follow-up counseling.

Milne is convinced that family self-determination provides a better solution to custody problems than could be achieved in court, where a judge may rely almost exclusively upon a mental health professional's recommendation. Moreover, parents who go to court for a decision usually go back to court within two years. Milne says that her system costs less and puts less stress on the family than does a litigated custody settlement.

Not every couple is capable of family self-determination. Some spouses want to punish each other. But for many troubled parents, family self-determination can lead to a positive result. And family courts generally are delighted to have custody questions resolved privately. Milne sent me a case to describe her process.

Jack and Doris Smith had been living apart for several years, after twenty-two years of marriage. They had three children, Dave (fifteen), Paula (thirteen), and Valeria (ten). Doris did not want a divorce. Jack was employed as a foreman in a printing plant. Doris had had problems with Dave and a psychologist had recommended that the boy live with Jack. The two girls had stayed with Doris.

The Smiths had been referred for a custody evaluation in their pending divorce action. The evaluator had recommended that they share legal custody, with the father having primary physical custody of the children. Later, this was amended to joint custody, based on a concern for sep-

arating the children from their mother. The Smiths asked
the court to refer their case to a privately employed custody mediator.

The primary issue was the custody of the girls; Doris
was willing to have her son live with Jack. Other concerns
needed to be confronted. Doris felt rejected. Her maternal
role was being threatened. Jack disapproved of Doris's
parenting style. He wanted to be in charge. Doris really
wanted a reconciliation.

Jack and Doris failed to reach an agreement even
though they participated in all the sessions and completed
the assigned tasks. Milne believes that Doris was using the
sessions to maintain her relationship with Jack and that
from the outset she had had no intention of reaching an
agreement: a settlement would have confirmed their separation. Doris used her attorney and her parents as excuses
for not agreeing with Jack. They were the true negotiators,
with Doris acting as their agent. Mediation failed.

Following the impasse, the parties returned to court.
Another custody evaluation was ordered. The investigator
recommended that Jack have legal custody of the children,
with physical custody shared. Following a two-day contested trial, the judge awarded legal custody to Jack with
visitation rights to Doris.

The mediation process covered nine sessions (roughly
ten hours). Parties were billed at an hourly rate of $35. No
estimate of court and legal costs is available.

Should a divorce mediator interview the children?

Under the AAA's Family Mediation Rules, a mediator may
interview a child privately to determine the child's attitude
toward custodial arrangements or visitation rights. Such an
interview can be arranged if both parties agree: "In conducting such an interview, the mediator should not encourage the child to choose between parents." The purpose of
the interview is to gain insight as to a workable plan for the

future. If the children prefer one arrangement over another, the mediator should be aware of their feelings.

Should children participate in the negotiations?

Children usually have no direct voice in the design of a separation agreement. In earlier days, they had nothing to say about the matter. At first the father was supreme; later, the mother achieved an equivalent voice. Now some judges will appoint an attorney for children in appropriate cases. In court, of course, the lawyers speak for their clients. The parents are not permitted to participate unless requested to do so by the court or asked to testify by their lawyer. That can be frustrating.

Mediation is flexible. The children can be invited to join in the discussion. Some mediators ask the children to read the draft agreement. It seems reasonable to be sure that the children understand and approve of an arrangement that will profoundly affect their lives. Of course, not every parent will want children to be involved in the negotiating process. Some adults don't like to share power with children. Moreover, whether children are able to take part in such discussions will depend upon their maturity. Even children who are thoughtful and articulate should not be involved in some circumstances. For instance, children should not be put in the position where their relationship with their parents might be jeopardized. A delicate judgment.

After a separation, children may become involved in family budgeting for the first time. The family will have to economize. Many divorced women learn to share concerns about money with their teenage children. When a mother has to earn money herself, that makes sense.

In general, I favor bringing children into mediation sessions. Their parents will be learning how to cope with the family's future. The children should also be exposed to some of these problems and help find solutions. Certainly, they have an interest in the results.

Does the mediator represent the children?

The mediator represents no one and does not take sides in the bargaining. At most, a mediator is expected to interpret the children's interests realistically to the parents. Many parents think of their children as possessions. At first, children may be viewed as symbolic property in a divorce. The parties and their lawyers argue over them, demanding child support, custody, or visitation in a macabre game of human chess. The mediator should convince parents that their children are real people, with feelings and wishes and rights. Above all, children have retentive memories.

Remember that even very young children understand that in divorce something is happening, something bad. They are all too willing to accept blame for their parents' breakup. They need to be convinced that they are not responsible. Children of divorced couples may carry emotional scars into their future lives. The mediator should try to guard against this happening.

What is a mediator's obligation toward an abused child?

Some parents abuse their children. They themselves may have been brought up in homes in which violence or verbal abuse was practiced. Child abuse is passed from generation to generation.

When child abuse is disclosed, what should a mediator do? First, find out the facts. Parents may talk freely about the harm they have done to their child. They may also describe the abuse that they themselves suffered as children. This is typical:

> I was brought up by my mother and my aunt. My mother would come home from work. When she was tired, she would

scream at me. Then my aunt would beat me. If I talked back, she would hit me across the face. I was afraid to tell anyone. Now, when things get out of hand, I get rough with the kid. Last week I punched the hell out of him. If I can't stop doing that, I could really hurt him. We could be in bad trouble. If my husband wasn't around, maybe it wouldn't happen.

This woman was in therapy. She thought that a divorce might reduce the stress that was causing her to abuse her child. The agency wasn't so sure. A volunteer, working with the family, believed that a separation would help. As her case report noted: "The husband seems to be a violent influence in that home. When he mistreats the wife, she takes it out on the child. She knows that she has a problem."

An abusive parent may still love the child. In mediation, parents may be able to work out a custodial arrangement that makes abuse less likely. Sometimes child abuse results from unusual, temporary stress in the family. Loss of a job is often cited as a cause: the parents are home too much, they are feeling hurt, and they have temporarily lost their self-respect. It is not surprising that they sometimes take these things out on their kids.

A mediator may conclude that placement with another family would be better for the child. There are no easy answers when dealing with child abuse, but family mediation is not necessarily out of the question in such cases.

Should a mediator consult with a mental health expert?

When custody questions arise in court, a judge is likely to request a professional opinion from a mental health specialist as to the best interests of the child. This may involve extensive interviews. The expert attempts to evaluate the parents' emotional stability. The children are asked about their relationship with each parent. Friends of the family and neighbors are also interviewed. This report may form the basis of the court's decision. Many parents don't like to be studied in this way. They would rather settle the custody question privately.

A mediator, of course, is not obligated to make such an investigation. If an arrangement is worked out through mediation, there may be no need for the investigation.

A mediator will help the parents consider various custodial alternatives, determining which formula best fits the needs of the children. Except in unusual circumstances, parents should not be forced to undergo an investigation.

Most parents bring up their children without outside intervention. Their right to decide what is best for their children should not be taken away from them because they are getting a divorce. However, when parents separate, their duties do need to be reallocated. In almost all cases, this can be done by the parents themselves. Of course, if the parents ask the mediator to obtain an outside professional opinion, this can easily be done.

Conclusion

The divorce mediator must work with clients who are apt to be antagonistic toward each other, particularly at the outset of the mediation. The mediator has an initial task of turning the parties away from their natural anger and toward a sensible readjustment for their future life. By rescuing couples from the danger of a contested divorce trial, the mediator can help them survive a potential crisis. The potential benefits to the children are discussed, coupled with an analysis of the options for child custody.

With or without children, couples who are able to negotiate a settlement are likely to find their divorce less painful than if they fought over the issues in the traditional way. A divorce mediator must be familiar with the kinds of problems that typically arise in a marital separation, although some mediators tend to specialize in one or another aspect of divorce.

4

How to Act as a Family Mediator

A MEDIATOR HELPS PEOPLE settle their disputes. That may sound simple, but in fact the process is extremely complicated. The mediator must persuade the parties that it is in their own interest to reach an agreement.

Being a family mediator is a thankless task. If parties make a mess of it, they blame the mediator. When parties finally settle, however, they take full credit for their success. The hard work of the mediator is forgotten. Since the entire process is private, no one will ever know how brilliantly the mediator brought the parties together.

Negotiating sessions often take place after the working day. A final settlement may be reached late in the evening, when the adversaries are willing to make the last few crucial concessions because they are worn out.

As one divorce mediator complained: "There are no easy cases. My clients are too caught up in their own problems and too embittered for mediation to be anything but a

hassle." Not everyone is willing to make such sacrifices
for other people. Most of us are fairly selfish. If you don't
have a keen interest in other people's problems, family
mediation may not be for you.

How does mediation differ from arbitration?

An arbitrator decides issues. A mediator, on the other
hand, must persuade the parties to settle their dispute. Mediation is used when people want to control their own negotiations. The mediator assists them, working directly
with the parties. Arbitration serves a different purpose.
When parties can't agree but don't want to go to court,
they can authorize an impartial arbitrator to make a binding
decision. Parties turn to arbitration when they are willing
to delegate decisionmaking power to a third person.

When substantial property interests are involved in a
divorce, the parties are likely to seek advice from attorneys. Here, too, there is a difference between arbitration
and mediation. In arbitration, the lawyers will present the
case to an arbitrator. Parties have a legal right to be represented by their attorneys. In mediation, the lawyers usually
serve as outside advisers. They are seldom present when
the mediation is taking place, although most mediators stay
in touch with the lawyers as the discussions develop.

Some therapists tout mediation as a way of keeping
lawyers out of the divorce process. That is wrong. Mediation is a technique for avoiding the adversarial approach
that lawyers are obliged to adopt. But many attorneys
serve as mediators. Some are quoted or identified in this
book.

Sometimes an individual will demand that an attorney
be present at mediation sessions to protect that party's
legal rights. Mediator Marsha Dorsky of New York handled that situation in one case by getting both parties to
agree that the lawyer could attend but would not speak on
behalf of the client without permission. The hearing could

be adjourned for a few minutes so that the lawyer could confer with the client. That arrangement worked reasonably well. The wife had wanted her attorney because she was afraid that she would not be able to express her thoughts. Her lawyer provided a sense of security. After one session, she felt comfortable with being on her own.

Because a mediator does not make decisions for the parties, there is seldom any need for an attorney to be present. In fact, that is a major difference between mediation and arbitration.

A mediator is not a judge

A mediator should never make a client feel guilty or blame one of the parties. The mediator should not appear to be judgmental.

This approach can pose difficulties for those of us who were trained as lawyers. Our entire career has involved identifying the guilty person, the party who is liable for damages. Lawyers are taught to assign responsibility. When lawyers serve as mediators, they have to take on a different attitude, reminding themselves not to make such judgments, taking the parties as they are, not as the lawyers might like them to be. One friend of mine who is a very fine trial lawyer frankly admitted that it would be impossible for him to be a mediator: "Every part of me has been programmed to take sides. Not a good characteristic, I suppose, but when for twenty years you have looked at issues as a partisan, you can't suddenly change."

What is a mediator expected to accomplish?

The mediator's goal is to persuade the parties to design a practical arrangement for their future, one that will survive. Both parties should be willing to abide by their agreement. The mediator must be reasonably certain that they will live by it. Also, the solution should be acceptable to other people who may be involved. The agreement must be viable: it is pointless to agree on something that doesn't work. One mediator put it this way: "Sometimes parties are stampeding for the barn. I have to stop them because they have not yet dealt with their problems. It takes time for people to rearrange their lives. I have to be sure that they have done their job."

Mediators soon realize that just because the clients have signed a document does not mean that a practical solution has been achieved. Unless the parties are committed to living under the arrangement, future events may provide them with ample opportunity to default from their obligations. An arbitration clause in the agreement may be a useful enforcement mechanism, but ultimately the parties must rely upon each other's good character.

What qualities are required of a family mediator?

A mediator must care what happens to the parties. That is crucial. There are other important criteria. A mediator must exhibit integrity and impartiality. Sensitivity is important. There's more. A mediator must be personally acceptable to a wide range of people, able to gain their confidence. A mediator has to be a skillful interviewer, good at digging out information. A mediator needs to be open-minded. People's problems take on a fascinating variety, reflecting the unique facets of our society.

A mediator must be able to lead people through the frustrations of the negotiating process. Accordingly, mediators need patience. Negotiations can get bogged down over trivial matters, and the parties must be allowed to rummage through such material at their own pace. Finally, the mediator should have a working knowledge of personal finances and of family law. Such knowledge comes from experience. As questions arise, a mediator may have to assemble various useful data. Family therapists, lawyers, social workers, or other experts may have to be consulted. Debt counseling can be important. The mediator must know more about such things than the parties: they will be looking to the mediator for useful advice.

A family mediator works on a very personal level. Listening carefully and identifying areas of compromise, the mediator must create a cooperative atmosphere. A mediator must be able to persuade the parties to agree, using whatever it takes to accomplish that task: "What can I tell you? It is hard, hard work. Sometimes I go home totally dejected, thinking that nothing has been accomplished. They spend the entire evening fighting with each other. Nothing comes together. I ask myself, 'What could I have done?' Other times, I feel in total control. It can be very frustrating or very satisfying, depending on what happens." This mediator has an excellent track record.

Skill and persistence are more important than personality. The mediator has to be able to bring parties together.

According to Harold Davis, a trainer with the Federal Mediation and Conciliation Service, "A mediator must be sensitive, skilled in communications, strong, logical, a capable problem-solver and have a keen sense of timing." Davis's judgment is based upon years of experience.

I know successful mediators who seem to have none of these characteristics. They are rude, insensitive, and not too bright. What good mediators seem to have in common is a strong desire to help parties solve problems. Is that compassion? Perhaps mediators are merely manipulative. Results are what count. If the parties are able to resolve their problems, mediation has been successful.

Mediators must acquire the ability to listen, turning off their own flow of thoughts in order to concentrate on what the clients are saying. An effective mediator acquires information like a sponge. Words, expressions, gestures, and even moments of silence provide clues about the parties. Pieced together, these elements form a meaningful pattern.

Can a lawyer serve as a family mediator?

Yes. But a lawyer-mediator neither offers legal advice nor provides representation to either party. An attorney may serve purely as a mediator.

Many leading lawyers support mediation. David R. Brink, while president of the American Bar Association, created the Special Committee on Alternative Means of Dispute Resolution to encourage mediation and arbitration. He urged lawyers to participate in such activities.

Many other bar leaders have encouraged the use of mediation. People do not like to be dragged into court. Clients become suspicious when lawyers encourage them to litigate. Thus, alternative dispute resolution has become a popular concept.

Many judges also encourage parties to settle their cases out of court. Indeed, a fair number of retired judges are eager to serve as arbitrators.

Is it ethical for a lawyer to mediate?

Some local bar associations sniff around their boundaries like guard dogs, snarling over the enforcement of codes of professional responsibility. Professor Linda J. Silberman, of New York University, has covered this subject in "Professional Responsibility: Problems of Divorce Mediation" (1981).

According to some bar associations, a lawyer should not mediate because legal advice should not be provided to parties who are in conflict. Some private mediation systems are challenged on that basis. A lawyer who combines mediation with the practice of divorce law may violate that policy. A lawyer-mediator who drafts a joint separation agreement may be caught in the same web.

Some states permit lawyers to represent both parties in a separation provided that, after full disclosure, the clients agree to use the lawyer. Other states do not permit dual representation.

A lawyer should be careful to differentiate between mediating and giving legal advice. A New York State ethics opinion lays it on the line: "A lawyer approached by a husband and wife in a matrimonial matter and asked to represent both may, however, properly undertake to serve as a mediator or arbitrator."

Both parties in a divorce case should be encouraged to consult their own attorneys. And any mediated agreement should be reviewed by independent counsel. Finally, a lawyer-mediator should not represent a party in subsequent legal proceedings.

The Association of the Bar of the City of New York has issued guidelines on mediation (1981). Both clients should be warned that important legal rights are involved in divorce. Parties should be encouraged to retain independent counsel to advise them about the potential risks. The City Bar's opinion does permit mediation by attorneys.

Some local bar associations still resist family mediation. That being so, a lawyer should stake out a narrow role when mediating and have the parties sign a retainer agreement both at the very beginning and at the conclusion of the mediation (as part of the final settlement).

The New York Court of Appeals recently refused to overturn a separation agreement negotiated by an attorney who had represented both parties. The lawyer was related to the husband by marriage and had represented him in some business deals. Nevertheless, the court in this case, *Levine* v. *Levine,* said that the lawyer had acted in a proper capacity:

> The record disclosed that the attorney had been an acquaintance of the husband and wife for a number of years. He agreed to draft the separation agreement only because the parties, prior to consulting him, already had reached an accord on the essential terms. Even then, the attorney told the wife that she could consult with another attorney, but the wife declined to do so.

Later the wife decided that she deserved more. She attacked the agreement, but without success.

According to the *Levine* decision, a New York lawyer can provide joint representation but must disclose any relationship with either of the clients. Then, if both parties are able to agree on the terms of the settlement, the lawyer can put their agreement in writing.

Shortly before *Levine* was decided in New York, the ethics committee of the Connecticut State Bar Association came to exactly the opposite conclusion (opinion issued on May 26, 1982). A lawyer should not draft a separation agreement for both parties, principally because conflicts of interest are all too likely to arise—in part because clients negotiating a divorce tend to be overly emotional. Thus, in the leading Connecticut case, *Kenworthy* v. *Kenworthy,* the wife claimed after the divorce that "she [had been] suffering from severe emotional distress which [had] rendered her incapable of understanding the words of the agreement." Moreover, the court was concerned that a lawyer who represents both parties in preparing a separation agreement may fail to obtain all the necessary information. The ethics committee felt that joint representation would be "indefensible." An attorney must make a choice: "In a separation agreement, a loss to one party directly corresponds to a gain to the other party."

Having ruled against joint representation, the Connecticut ethics committee went on to take an enlightened position on mediation. If a lawyer discloses all present or former relationships with the parties, impartial service as a mediator is acceptable. But the mediator should not represent either party in any subsequent dispute. A lawyer-mediator should be "careful not to render legal advice to either or both parties under these circumstances."

Bar committees in Florida, Maryland, Massachusetts, and Ohio permit joint representation. But be careful! Your clients already hate each other. They may fall into the hands of lawyers who are hostile to mediation.

Can a lay mediator give legal advice?

A nonlawyer serving as a family mediator must be particularly careful not to provide legal advice. It may be necessary to discuss family law, but the mediator should not advise the parties. One of the clients, unhappy about the settlement, may later say that the mediator suggested a particular legal solution. Then some lawyer may complain that the mediator was practicing law.

A divorce mediator should be familiar with family law. It is unrealistic to think that such knowledge will not be shared with the parties. Parties ask questions. The mediator is expected to answer. Be careful. Recognize the risk. A hostile bar association may claim that you were practicing law. A lay mediator can protect against liability by telling the parties at the outset not to expect legal advice. Parties should be advised to rely on their own lawyers.

Can a mediator be totally impartial?

We all have our biases, sometimes quite unsuspected ones. A mediator may undervalue someone of the opposite sex, of a different generation, or of an alien culture. A mediator should try to overcome such prejudices but may nevertheless find it impossible to work with particular parties.

To resolve this problem, the Northwest Mediation Service in Oregon, founded by Stephen Gaddis and Alice Probert in 1977, developed a team practice. Gaddis is an attorney. Probert is a social worker. They believe that in divorce mediation, one mediator should be male, the other female. Probert and Gaddis think that two mediators of opposite sexes can offer a broader, more impartial service. For example, they say that one mediator should be a lawyer and the other should be a mental health specialist.

The Gaddis-Probert idea is that no one profession is competent to handle all the subtleties of family mediation —lawyers "are not trained in how to deal with family and marital dynamics''; nonlawyers can't understand legal concepts. I don't agree. An intelligent mediator can acquire multidisciplinary skills. A mediator's sex or professional training does not necessarily determine whether the mediator will be fair to both parties or will gain their confidence. Indeed, a family mediator has enough to worry about without having to coordinate efforts with those of a co-mediator. My preference is to use a single mediator, one selected with the particular case in mind. If the issues are primarily behavioral, pick a therapist or a social worker. If the dispute concerns property, select a lawyer or a financial planner.

Other family mediation centers have adopted the team model. This is O.K. Only after the mediation process matures can an intelligent appraisal be made of the various options.

How does the team work?

Combining a lawyer and a therapist as a team does avoid some of the problems faced by a single mediator. A team, based in Armonk, New York, involves a psychologist, Dr. John J. Shaw, and an attorney, Naomi Matusow. Under their system, the first meeting with the clients is a joint consultation with both partners. At the second session, Shaw gives the parties a kit containing budget forms and descriptions of the various options for child custody and division of marriage property. The couple then meets with Matusow, who helps them discuss their legal rights. When an issue is identified, it is worked out with Shaw.

This is an interesting approach. The lawyer serves as traffic manager, defining the issues and providing technical information. The psychologist helps the parties come to an agreement. As Shaw points out, ''There are real issues and symbolic issues. Money is a terribly important issue in marriage. Objects may be real or may be symbolic. One person may seem rigid about a particular possession, say, a car. What does it mean? It may represent a cherished memory, or it may represent an opportunity to punish the other person.''

Shaw believes that adolescent children deserve to be heard: "Their needs and feelings should be recognized. The family is being reorganized, not disbanded. The parents should be encouraged to continue to relate to their children. This opportunity should not be lost.''

The Shaw-Matusow system takes about a dozen hour-long sessions. The cost of the service averages $1,200, split about equally between the psychologist and the attorney. Any agreement is reviewed by the parties' attorneys before being signed. This team has avoided ethical and legal problems by allocating responsibilities carefully.

A somewhat more customized approach has been adopted by the Divorce Mediation Center in Old Greenwich, Connecticut, run by Dr. Richard G. Abell, a psychiatrist, Patricia Kane, a lawyer, and Joseph M. Dowling, an accountant. According to Kane, "We are tending to see the more affluent, educated people, but mediation is suitable for every income level. People don't want to spend a lot of money on fees, but they want a divorce with dignity." Costs for mediation at the Abell center run from $1,500 to $3,500 for average cases. The couple's problems are resolved in a series of up to ten two-hour sessions, which focus on tax planning, property settlement, and child custody and support. Again, the agreement is reviewed by the parties' personal lawyers.

Mediation centers using a team approach must meet the requirements of local professional practice committees. Otherwise, the lawyer on the team may be charged with joint representation and the therapist may be accused of practicing law. A lawyer is expected to report unauthorized practice. A lawyer may not practice law in association with a nonlawyer. Fee splitting or sharing of clients is prohibited. If a mediation team drafts a separation agreement and then goes on to obtain a divorce for the parties, the team members may be in violation on several counts.

Another potential problem arises when a lawyer serves on the staff of a mediation center. Lawyers are not supposed to permit a lay agency to intervene between themselves and their clients. Serving as a mediator is not practicing law. Some bar associations may not accept that distinction. Some agencies have tried to solve this riddle by putting lawyers firmly in charge of the service, with lay mediators working as paraprofessionals. Therapists may resist that approach. It will be interesting to see how these problems are resolved.

Is a family mediator likely to be sued?

The risk of a lawsuit is always present. A mediator can protect against legal liability by emphasizing the difference between mediation and acting as an attorney. That will reduce the risk.

Still, a family mediator is dealing with distressed people. They can't get along. They may detest each other. The mediator should be careful not to get caught in their squabbles. The chairman of the Family Law Section of the American Bar Association, Samuel V. Schoonmaker III, cautions: "If somebody feels they lost out because the mediator was not doing his job, they will sue for malpractice."

The attorneys for the parties also may be eager to find fault with the mediation and may try to hold the mediator accountable. For protection, the mediator should establish friendly relationships with clients' attorneys. Of course, this is not foolproof: new lawyers may come into the picture.

In a 1981 Missouri case, *Lange* v. *Marshall,* a wife filed a lawsuit against her lawyer-mediator on the ground that her support was inadequate. She had retained a new lawyer and had threatened to sue her former husband, with the result that the husband agreed to increase his support payments. The Missouri court dismissed her claim against the mediator. The wife could not prove that her husband would have offered more money in the earlier negotiations.

Some courts have held that mediators are immune from liability, but this issue has not been tested in every state. Rule 14 of the AAA's Family Mediation Rules says that the mediator may not be held liable for performing in that capacity. This should be explained to the parties. To be doubly certain, a family mediator should obtain a waiver of liability before accepting the case. This waiver should be incorporated into the final settlement.

Is there any physical danger involved in being a mediator?

A mediator works with people who may hate each other. Once in a while, a client will direct anger at the mediator. Watch out when that happens.

A mediator should be careful not to provoke the parties. Don't establish a close personal relationship with either client. The other is likely to be suspicious. The mediator must merit the parties' continuing trust.

Some practical suggestions:

- Don't serve liquor or permit the use of any drugs during sessions.

- Don't let mediation sessions turn into a party.

- Don't date or go to bed with a client.

- Don't allow your clients to indulge in excessive name calling.

- Don't continue meeting when one of the parties seems distraught.

- Don't condone a physical threat by either party.

- Keep sessions cool and businesslike.

Some couples have a habit of fighting. Don't indulge them. Arguments can get out of control. At the very least, they are disruptive.

Family mediation is not particularly dangerous, but be cautious. More police officers are injured in family fights than in armed robberies. Ask your local cop about domestic violence.

Must a family mediator be a professional?

Divorce mediation may become a profession. Not yet. At present, anyone can become a family mediator. The trick is to get clients. As Professor Silberman puts it, "Anybody can hang out a shingle and say 'I'm a mediator.' " Watch out for quacks!

A mediator must know something about family law. In addition, a competent mediator should be an expert in financial planning, family counseling, and mediation techniques. The problem is how to obtain such knowledge and how to acquire experience.

Larry Ray, director of the American Bar Association's Special Committee on Alternative Means of Dispute Resolution, has said that there seems to be little difference in ability between "professionals with a lengthy training in mediation theory and technique" and "lay people from the community." As he points out, it all depends upon the case that is being resolved.

Some mediations can be quite casual. One purpose of this book is to encourage readers to practice informal mediation on that basis. Mediation can help to resolve day-to-day family problems. Give it a try. Act as a mediator within your own family. At the very least, you will increase your family's communicating skills.

I am not that cavalier about more complex cases. Obviously, divorce mediators get involved in substantial personal and property interests. They should be experts and should maintain high professional standards. The Family

Law Section of the American Bar Association and other interested groups are working on a code of ethics for divorce mediators. We see a continuing need for training and for increasing the level of competence of mediators.

If one party is a better negotiator, what should the mediator do?

A mediator is impartial in a very special sense. The goal of mediation is to help the parties reach a sound settlement. Time will tell whether that goal has been achieved. The agreement has to provide a framework for the parties' future lives. Whether it represents a lasting solution depends upon the contingencies of future years. Separation agreements are fragile documents. The family mediator can only hope that they will survive. What the parties learn about themselves during the discussions may be more meaningful in the long run than whatever words are contained in the formal document.

In family mediation, the parties are seldom exactly equal. Perfect balance may not be possible. The family mediator may have to equalize the parties.

Mediator John Hayes recommends that mediators attempt to maintain an equilibrium between the parties, sometimes persuading one to retreat from an unreasonable position or encouraging a more assertive approach by the other: "Balance is achieved by adhering to the broad principle that the mediator is not committed to either party but to the final agreement."

Mediators should ask hard questions before the bargaining begins:

- Are the parties ready to negotiate?
- Do I know enough about their problem?
- Have both parties identified their goals?

- Are they competent to confront each other?

- Will the interests of third persons be protected?

True neutrality is being able to answer such questions in the affirmative. Unless both parties are reasonably prepared to negotiate, the system will not be fair.

Where can a mediator get training?

A jurisdictional dispute has been emerging in the area of mediation. According to *American Family,* a struggle over professional turf has been shaping up: "The American Bar Association has taken the position that lawyers are the appropriate mediators in court related problems. On the other hand, the Association of Family Conciliation Courts trains primarily behavioral scientists, drawn from the ranks of court personnel."

I believe that any qualified person should be free to serve as a family mediator, mediating with friends or relatives or, if qualified, offering mediation as a supplement to other professional activities. I do appreciate the need for specialized training for handling more complicated situations such as divorce.

One experienced family mediator, Mark Lohman of Washington, has said, "The educational needs of a mediator are highly complex. Not only must the mediator have a knowledge of family law almost comparable to that of a family lawyer, but [the mediator] must be knowledgeable in family therapy issues, especially the impact of divorce on children. One must know about taxes, as well as present-day and long-term finances, including health and life insurance."

Several organizations already provide training in family mediation. The programs include mock mediation sessions, supplemented by lectures on substantive areas. Custody problems and the financial aspects of family law are usually covered. This kind of training does not produce a fully accomplished family mediator, nor does it create a work-load for the trainees. But it does help acquire and maintain some competence in the field.

Appendix C outlines a three-day training seminar of-fered from time to time by the American Arbitration As-sociation. The newly formed Academy of Family Mediators also provides a basic training program, as well as advanced seminars for practitioners (the tuition for the basic course is $600).

The academy points out that it is important to ask how many programs a particular training facility has carried out. Are the trainers experienced mediators? What have they published on the subject? What model do they encourage? Is there a strong local group for follow-up training and supervision? These questions should be asked before sign-ing up for any training program.

An interesting training program is offered by Family Mediation of Greater Washington, which also provides me-diation services. Phase one of the program gives the partic-ipant an initial understanding of the process, including mediation theory and ethical considerations. Demonstra-tions and role-plays are also included. Phase two involves independent study, consisting of assignments provided by the training staff over a period of three to five months. Trainees have an opportunity to observe and participate in mediation sessions conducted at the center. Phase three integrates and applies mediation skills by emphasizing the techniques used in various models. It takes place in a con-centrated period of seven days. Phase four is a career-long process of working with experienced mediators and con-sulting with members of the center staff. The training staff are family law attorneys with experience in mediation. The co-directors are Patricia E. Shahen and Professor Law-rence D. Gaughan; both are affiliated with the Academy of Family Mediators.

Can mediation be obtained without charge?

Sometimes mediation is free. The mediator may be a friend
of the family and therefore willing to serve without compensation. Or mediation may be offered as a free service
by a social agency.

The most rapidly growing mediation service is found in
the conciliation departments of family courts and is provided without charge. For example, a special commission
in Massachusetts recommended that "nonadversarial dispute resolution should be available in every probate and
family court as an option for the many families that can
benefit from such an alternative process."

In spite of being free, these services can be of high
quality. Paul S. Kaufman directs the Court Mediation Services in Framingham, Massachusetts. His office provides
free mediation to parties referred by the court. Kaufman
sent me a case that he handled with a co-mediator.

The case involved a wife who was seeking a temporary
restraining order against her husband to get him out of the
marital home. The couple had been married for fourteen
years. They had been separated once before, some six
years earlier. The husband was self-employed and operated
a small business. The wife was employed part-time as a
school-bus driver. There were three children, aged six,
nine, and twelve.

Both parties had been interviewed by the agency's case
coordinator to establish that their situation was appropriate
for mediation and to obtain their agreement to participate.
The mediators learned that the disputants argued continu-
ously over money. They showed little understanding of
each other's needs.

The initial session with the disputants got bogged down,
so the mediators met with the husband and the wife separately, patiently listening as they talked about their frustrations. The mediators expressed sympathy because both
parties seemed to be under great stress. Finally, they were
brought together to discuss the issues.

When an impasse was reached, the mediators met with the case coordinator. This was helpful in allowing the mediators to view the problems objectively and to identify alternative solutions for the disputants. A key issue was the problem of abusive telephone calls from the husband. This was resolved by scheduling specific times for calls to be made by the husband to the children. The husband agreed to pay a deposit into the mediation office. If he continued making such calls, the telephone number would be changed. The money would be turned over to the wife to pay for the change. The money would revert to the husband in ninety days if the arrangement was successful.

The issues of support and visitation were incorporated in a written agreement that the parties signed and that the mediators approved and witnessed. After abiding by the agreement for a year, while their divorce was pending, the couple decided to live together again.

California and several other states require conciliation in divorces that involve child custody. The mediators are either salaried government employees or state-paid consultants. The service is free to the parties.

What do private mediators charge?

In mediation cases that require experience and special knowledge, a private mediator would expect to be compensated. Most divorce mediators practice on a fee-for-service basis. The terms of payment should be arranged when the relationship is established. Since family mediation is relatively new, few guidelines exist as to what to expect. A mediator may charge an hourly or a daily fee. Some portion of the fee may be payable in advance.

Divorce mediators charge anywhere from $20 to $100 per hour, depending upon their professional credentials and the community in which they practice.

Family mediators are seldom paid as well as successful practicing attorneys, although some attorney-mediators report that they are able to charge their usual hourly rates for mediation. Mediation is time-consuming and emotionally exhausting. Considering the stress, family mediation is not an easy road to riches. It is hard work and probably will never yield lucrative fees.

What does a mediator have to know?

The parties will have to gather various types of information before they can reach a settlement. The mediator should have a general knowledge of family law. Family mediators tell me that each case requires them to explore a new area.

Probably, a family mediator should practice within a reasonably familiar environment. The relationships between husbands and wives and their children can be quite different in some cultures. A mediator might have difficulty working with people from another ethnic or racial group. Even generational gaps may be hard to surmount.

Among immigrant families, children often serve as a bridge between the adult members of the family and the community. Sometimes they actually mediate. In a rapidly changing society, young people often help their parents cope with wrenching readjustments. Traditionally, mediators were recruited from among the elders. Now the generations are sometimes turned upside-down.

Some older people find it difficult to mediate when the authority of a parent is being challenged by an adolescent: "I could not believe what I was hearing. When I was a girl, we were never permitted to question a decision made by our parents. Here I was, listening to that little tramp calling her father a fool, calling him names in front of her mother and her little brother. I could hardly keep my temper."

Do mediators have to travel?

People constantly relocate. It is not unusual for one of the parties to move to another community. Mediation usually requires face-to-face discussions. This presents a practical problem. The mediator must figure out how to bring the parties together. While useful talks can be carried out on the telephone, long distance, a direct confrontation may be required.

In general family mediation takes place in the community in which the family is located. As a mediator's reputation grows, more travel may be required. Some mediators shuttle back and forth between parties residing far apart. Lawyers serving wealthy clients think nothing of jetting around the world. A few family mediators may develop a similar practice, but most will continue to work in their local communities.

Should a mediator know about employment problems?

Most family income comes from employment. Sometimes, to resolve a dispute, someone will have to find a job or switch careers to generate more income. That is often true for women after a divorce. A divorce mediator should be familiar with the local employment market, the state unemployment compensation system, and other forms of government assistance. Such expertise will help the mediator serve as a problem-solver.

In other kinds of family disputes, employment concerns may be less obvious. But most families are supported by wages or salaries. The wage earner will have a veto over whatever is negotiated. If that person stops working, the money stops. If the money is diverted, the agreement breaks down. If the worker gets sick or dies, all bets are off.

Do mediators need to be familiar with tax laws?

A mediator should have a working knowledge of the tax laws. Often, an innovative solution to a dispute may involve figuring out how certain funds can be handled most advantageously. The family mediator should be able to spot potential tax problems and should know when to recommend that the parties obtain tax advice.

Few Americans use tax advisers. Usually they rely on whoever helps them with their tax returns, perhaps a relative knowledgeable about taxes. Some mediators combine mediation with a knack for reducing the cost of the settlement by innovative tax planning. This may make it easier for the parties to reach an agreement. New York attorney Adriane Berg's mediation technique involves exactly that approach. Her cases are interesting because they show how financial planning can help overcome a couple's emotional concerns on the way to a final agreement. Here is an example.

The parties were fighting over whether their son could continue to go to private school. The tuition was $3,000 per semester. The mother wanted him to stay but could not afford the tuition. The father insisted that the boy go to a public school. No compromise seemed possible: either the child went to private school or he did not.

Berg encourages a problem-solving approach. Communication flows freely between the parties and the mediator during the joint sessions. She calls this the "triangle method" because everyone works together in the sessions to come to an agreement. Clients are urged to express their feelings and their concerns. Sometimes their initial positions have little to do with their real interests. What they say they want is not necessarily what they really want.

In this case, the mediator learned that the father did not really object to a private school: He didn't want to pay the total cost. More important, he wanted to help choose the school. Once this became clear, the next step was obvious. The mediator suggested that each parent have an equal say in the selection of a school. At first, the parties rejected her suggestion. After a long discussion, they finally agreed to talk over the choice of a private school; however, the father would make the final decision since he was paying most of the tuition. This satisfied him. It also was acceptable to the mother, who respected his judgment.

Berg then assumed the role of tax consultant. By reallocating the support payments already agreed upon, she increased the husband's tax deductions. The result was that he received a tax benefit of $4,500 per year. Therefore, the cost of private school after taxes was approximately $1,500 a year, rather than $6,000.

What role does religion play in mediation?

Each religion has its own rules about the family. An outsider may not understand these. Consequently, a mediator from the parties' own faith may be more comfortable with concerns that relate to religious teachings. But people marry across religious lines, and many couples look outside their religion for help. A mediator may prefer, therefore, not to try to deal with religious issues.

Some religions offer their own brand of mediation. The Christian Legal Society of Oakland, Illinois, maintains several conciliation centers. One is run by attorney Laurence Eck in Albuquerque. His center has resolved hundreds of cases, many referred by churches. Using traditional mediation techniques, the team includes a lawyer, a church leader, and a specialist in the problem; in a family separation, for example, the third member may be a marriage counselor or a psychiatrist. The mediators work with the parties much as they would in a secular program. The parties are encouraged to take responsibility for their own lives. Secular mediators preach the same message. As Eck told a newspaper reporter, there are no patented procedures in peacemaking.

How does a mediator get cases?

Like any personal service, family mediation must be marketed.

Attorney Henry M. Elson of Berkeley, California, after practicing law for seventeen years, decided to create a family law practice "outside of the adversary system." He became a divorce mediator. Cases were referred to him by fellow attorneys, therapists, counselors, and friends. His service was publicized in newspaper and magazine articles.

Many family courts offer mediation services. As we have seen, in California, mediation is required in divorce cases that involve children. The Conciliation Court Law was enacted in 1969 as Code of Civil Procedure, sections 1730–1772. Several other states have similar laws.

Increasing numbers of private divorce mediation centers are being established. Some are mentioned in this book. Others are listed in the Yellow Pages. The Academy of Family Mediators is trying to establish a network of local councils. If successful, these councils will be able to recommend mediators who are qualified members of the academy.

Some mediators receive cases from attorneys. After property and support issues have been resolved, an attorney might ask a mediator to help the parties settle the custody problem.

Of course, most family disputes don't come to mediation. Kids run away from home. Parents squabble. The family is in trouble, but no one wants to intervene. Friends realize that there is a problem but decide that they can't do anything about it. In such situations, someone should recommend that the problem be mediated. Likewise, schools, social agencies, and hospitals should either recommend mediation or offer such services when the situation warrants. We say that the family is a crucial part of our society. Why not invest in it?

The American Arbitration Association is another potential source of referrals. For example, New Jersey mediator James B. Boskey was appointed to a case by the AAA. The couple had heard Boskey talking about mediation on WABC radio, but they wanted to contact him through a reference agency. The case is interesting in itself. It was primarily a business transaction.

The couple, in their mid-fifties, had been married for almost twenty-five years. They had no children. They had separated recently but were on reasonably good terms, communicating about twice a week. The separation came about when the husband had moved in with a girlfriend, but this was not his first extramarital affair. The wife continued to live in their house.

The husband was employed by New York State and was earning $30,000 per year. He had no assets except a pension, a car, and part ownership of the marital home. He was deeply in debt, $18,000 of which he owed his wife. She was employed as a part-time legal secretary, earning a modest salary; in addition, she had about $40,000 remaining from an inheritance. They both wanted a divorce. She was not asking for support and they had agreed on everything except for sharing their interest in the house and paying off his debt to her.

At the first mediation session, the parties were encouraged to talk about the issues. They could agree on the value of the house, which had been appraised, and they knew the current value of the mortgage. The house was worth $64,000. The outstanding principal was $11,000. The wife wanted the equity in the house to be divided in half. She would keep the house and pay her husband's share, less the amount of his debt. This would have involved a payment of about $5,000. The husband agreed that the equity be divided in half, but he wanted to receive credit for payments he had made on the mortgage while they were still living together and for the rent he had paid before they purchased the house. Under his proposal, he would receive $26,500. The mediator tried to explain that neither position could be fully justified. Any number of formulas could be used to divide the interest in the house.

The second session began with both parties complaining that the mediator had "put down" their ideas. The mediator encouraged them to discuss the problem across the table. The husband said that he would take $13,000. The wife, however, stayed with her initial offer.

The third session concentrated on minor issues such as the maintenance of insurance. The parties were able to agree on everything except the basic issue. The mediator asked them to come to the next session ready to discuss the house.

At the fourth session, the mediator pointed out that money was the only outstanding issue. The parties began to bargain. After a series of offers and counteroffers, it was agreed that the wife would pay $8,500. The husband would transfer his interest in the house. The wife would forgive his debts. The money would be paid when the divorce was final. A summary of the agreement was discussed with the mediator to be certain that the parties understood the arrangement. The wife would draft a final agreement, drawing on her experience as a legal secretary. That document would be reviewed by counsel for both parties and put in final form. This being done, the mediation was terminated.

The mediation took five sessions, averaging ninety minutes each. The parties paid an hourly fee to the mediator, totaling about $450. Each party paid an attorney to review the agreement. The wife's counsel put through the divorce.

Since the American Arbitration Association is well known for its commercial arbitration service, many of these kinds of property- or business-related domestic disputes are likely to come to its attention. For those sorts of controversies, the AAA may become a major referral service. But various other agencies will come to play a similar role: receiving requests for family mediators and referring them to qualified professionals.

Many communities already are establishing mediation services. Larry Hyde, executive director of the Association of Family Conciliation Courts, says that "mediation's time has come."

In some communities, these services handle minor criminal complaints. Often, family conflicts are at the heart of such cases. These centers tend to serve a low-income segment of the population. They rely on government grants and volunteer mediators. Unfortunately, many people don't know such services exist.

Should corporations encourage family mediation?

The personal problems of employees have an effect upon their productivity. Some corporations help employees with such concerns. This is done either through the personnel department or through outside consultants. Corporations also should offer family mediation. But how? Why not maintain a list of reliable family mediators? Corporations could identify a local family mediation center as a resource or ask the American Arbitration Association for a list of recommended family mediators.

Conclusion

The reader who decides to act as a family mediator or to take on that role as a professional will have some practical questions, many of which were answered in this chapter. A mediator does not have to be a member of any particular profession, but if the mediator is a lawyer, certain ethical questions must be dealt with. The mediator should neither represent either party nor give legal advice. At the same time, the mediator must be generally familiar with the law and various other subject areas. Since no one person is likely to be an expert in all such fields, some mediators work as a team. These and other problems involved in the practice of family mediation were described in some detail. Finally, the need and availability of appropriate training were discussed.

5

Family Disputes and the Law

As we have seen, a mediator needs a working knowledge of family law's peculiarities, enough to explain them to the parties. There is a difference between discussing the law and giving a legal opinion. Mediators sometimes are asked for legal advice on a range of matters. They must resist any temptation to give it. One lawyer, trying his wings as a mediator, offered an unsolicited opinion on federal tax law. The client sued after discovering that the advice was erroneous. That is the danger. If the mediator had simply pointed out the problem and encouraged the parties to talk to their tax advisers, he would have been all right.

In this chapter, I describe some basic aspects of family law of which any mediator should be aware. Remember, however, family law is changing—and changing very rapidly. As Doris Freed pointed out in her overview of family law in the September 28, 1982, *Family Law Reporter,* "Family law remains unpredictable. The difficulty is that the solution of one problem merely generates additional ones.'' Of course, in general, the legal rights of women have expanded. Women have achieved some remarkable victories and some equally notable defeats. Many traditional doctrines are now obsolete. Marriage itself has changed. In the Victorian family, the husband was dominant. He "owned" the family. No longer. Some husbands think the tables have turned. In fact, that issue is still in doubt.

Marriage and the family continue to play an important role in our culture. We seldom consider how much we depend upon these institutions to stabilize society. The court cases that I will be discussing are often attempts to protect children's interests and to serve the economic and social needs of the family unit and, in turn, of society.

What is unique about marriage?

Increasing numbers of adults are living alone or attempting to cope with the demands of parenthood without a partner. But millions more are getting married. Admittedly, many people plunge into marriage with only a casual thought for the consequences. They learn. Oh, do they learn!

Marriage is a compact between two people, a special kind of contract. Consider the following:

- Almost any adult has the legal capacity to get married.

- Marriage creates a unique legal status.

- It creates many legal rights and obligations that can't be transferred or assigned.

- It is permanent. It can be dissolved only by death or by a court of competent jurisdiction.

People wonder why it is so easy to get married but so difficult to get divorced. The answer should be obvious.

The state has an equity interest in encouraging stable marriages because the income provider accepts responsibility for the spouse and for any offspring of their union. The state relieves itself of responsibility. No wonder any prudent government makes it easy to marry and erects barriers to divorce. This policy has been a solid success in the United States. Family law varies slightly from state to state, but everywhere marriage is easier to get into than to get out of. The income producer feeds the drones. In most families, the husband still supports his wife and children.

What are the rights of women in marriage?

Under traditional Anglo-Saxon law, a married woman had restricted legal rights. She could not enter into contracts. She could neither sue nor be sued. She could not vote or hold public office. Her personal property became the property of her husband. If she wanted to engage in business, she had to operate as her husband's agent, using her husband's credit and holding property in her husband's name. She was like property herself.

Some people continue to live by such rules. A few. Men think of their wives and children as property. Women submit. Children suffer pangs of guilt when they challenge parental authority. These traditional attitudes are important in our approach toward family problems.

Older women may recall how much lobbying was required before their sex won even the most basic legal rights. Women have come a long way, step by step. The Married Women's Property Act was a radical revision of the legal structure. The Nineteenth Amendment, giving the vote to women, was as shocking in its time as the Civil Rights Act was in ours. Women had to fight in order to achieve their present status. Now American women have more freedom and greater rights than ever before.

Of course, the battle goes on. Total equality has not yet been achieved. Tension exists between women who want

absolute freedom and those who hold more traditional
views. Cultural attitudes are difficult to change. A family
mediator soon learns that people's attitudes are not always
in step with the times. Most families don't operate on the
basis of individual equality. Plenty of men expect to dominate their wives and children. Many housewives live just
as they would have in Victorian times, except that they
don't have servants and may be encouraged to go out and
get a job.

How has family law changed?

Some people no longer believe that marriage is forever.
Divorce has become more acceptable. People who get divorced don't think of themselves as pariahs.

A stigma used to be attached to divorce. The courts
tried to identify which partner was responsible and to punish the so-called culprit. Divorce laws are less judgmental
today: "incompatibility" or "irretrievable breakdown" are
now acceptable grounds for divorce. Couples who have
been living apart for a certain period of time qualify for
what's called a "no-fault divorce." As Professor Sanford
Katz put it in a 1981 article in the *National Law Journal,* it
is now possible "to dissolve a marriage that is not function-
ing well, without making a charade of the adversary process."

The paternal judge who based decisions on natural law
and dispensed moral wisdom is long gone. Today family
judges are more likely to turn to Freud than to the Scrip-
tures for guidance. They rely upon family therapists rather
than their personal experience as fathers. The gestalt has
changed. Clinical concepts are used to appraise the child's
needs.

Even this may be changing. The court's concern for the
best interests of the child is being expanded to cover other
social values, such as the preservation of the family and

the autonomy of the individual parents. Family law has become increasingly complicated as government agencies and their advisers intervene in family arrangements. Society is no longer based on simple homilies and traditional morality.

What is the role of family court?

In the divorce process, a court of family jurisdiction has authority to approve separation agreements and to grant divorce decrees. If the parties are unable to resolve their dispute amicably, they may be forced to submit to the judgment of a family court judge armed with the compulsory powers of the state. This unattractive prospect motivates many parties to bargain privately.

A mediator should become familiar with family court procedures. By attending trials, a mediator can gain a working understanding of how cases are resolved in court. With even a modicum of such exposure it should not be difficult to persuade clients that courts are not the best place to work out personal problems.

Mediation is preferable for the reasons I listed earlier. The parties maintain control. Mediation is voluntary. The sessions are private and informal. The parties can build a new, cooperative relationship. Most clients understand that a contested lawsuit would strain whatever good feelings they still have about each other.

Even when some effort is made to create an atmosphere of relative informality, court trials become a pitched battle between the lawyers. Experts play an important role. Some psychologists and therapists say that courts put too much weight upon expert opinions. One court expert put it this way:

> When I establish my professional credentials in court and then pontificate about what I think might be best for a child, I sometimes become alarmed because the judge has no other

basis for a decision. I am controlling the case. My judgment is being imposed upon that family, a sobering idea. What do I know about what they want to make of themselves? How do they really feel about their kids? I wish that I could sit down with them and take the time to talk about it. The system doesn't work that way.

Through family courts and social service agencies, the state intervenes in the family, attempting to regulate the lives of children and adults. Sometimes these proceedings harm the individuals and their relationships. The adversary process requires parties to take polarized positions, which prolongs the conflict. The process itself produces legal costs and even more antagonism. This is particularly true of contested custody cases. Some intended reforms, such as assigning a lawyer to the child, may increase the delays and costs of the process.

When a child is removed from home by court action, parents believe that they have failed. They may be denied access to the child. Government support payments are reduced. They no longer control the child. The parents end up feeling worthless. Often they *have* failed, but in other cases the ruling may have been based on cultural differences, perhaps friction between a white middle-class social worker and a poor black unmarried mother. Similarly, parent's ineptitude may be caused by unemployment, poor health, or despair, rather than by lack of love for the child.

When a child is institutionalized or placed in foster care, a family may be destroyed forever. Foster care provides a good example. Many children are temporarily removed from the home for undetermined periods, with scant hope of ever returning. Little is done to rehabilitate the natural parents. However, when the time comes to cut off the rights of the natural parents so that the child can be put up for adoption, the court expresses concern about the rights of the biological family. Thousands of foster children and their parents thus remain in limbo. Again the family is diminished.

Opportunities for court intervention in family life are

extensive. There are over one million divorces each year. Two-thirds of these involve young children. Over half a million children are in foster care. Part of the problem has to do with parents who are not ready for parenthood. One out of five fourteen-year-old girls becomes pregnant. When they seem irresponsible, important decisions are made by courts and are justified on the basis of professional opinions rather than the preferences of the family involved. Unfortunately, the control systems are often in opposition. The law may impose an adversary process upon family disputes. At the same time, social service agencies offer counseling and treatment. When both systems focus on a family, a curious mishmash results. Sometimes it is difficult to forecast the result. For example, lawyers often ask judges to consider the child's "need for permanence" or "need for a psychological parent." What does that jargon mean to real people?

What are the grounds for divorce?

When courts could grant divorces solely on the basis of fault, one party would accuse the other of adultery, desertion, physical or mental cruelty, or nonsupport. Now that has changed.

State legislatures concluded that fault-oriented divorce laws did not discourage married couples from seeking divorces. Judges reported that such laws encouraged parties to commit perjury in obtaining a divorce. Some lawyers would write a scenario in advance for proving adultery, hiring prostitutes who would be "discovered" in a motel room with the "guilty" spouse. This was demeaning to the judges and, of course, to the attorneys and their clients, who sometimes found themselves embroiled in a public scandal.

The Uniform Divorce Act provided a new approach. The court now has to determine that a marriage is irretrievably broken. This can be done either by demonstrating that the parties have lived apart for more than 180 days or by proving that a serious discord exists between the parties. In some jurisdictions, the court may require conciliation, an effort to reconcile the parties.

As no-fault concepts gained acceptance, courts attempted to circumvent the rigid statutes. Now most state laws provide for no-fault divorce. But there is great variety. Some states kept the old grounds but added on the new. Thus, a mediator should be familiar with the particular state law.

- Some states accept incompatibility as a ground for divorce.

- Some require the parties to live apart for a certain period of time, perhaps one or two years.

- Others require the parties to demonstrate an irretrievable breakdown of the marriage.

Couples who meet the statutory requirements can come to court for a divorce decree when they have agreed on the terms of their separation. A hearing may be required, but not to determine who was at fault. The judge will want to know whether the separation agreement was entered into voluntarily and is in the public interest.

In general, most Americans agree that dead marriages should be terminated, that family assets should be fairly divided, that equitable support payments should be made, and that the children should continue to associate with their parents. But how to apply those principles to the facts of a particular case?

State divorce laws address such issues as property allocation, alimony, and child support. For example, property acquired during the marriage will be divided in accordance with a formula, unless a different agreement has been entered into by the parties. The local law on these subjects should be studied carefully.

What are the ramifications of a no-fault divorce?

Under no-fault divorce, the court has broad discretion. If the parties come to court with a negotiated separation agreement, judges usually grant a divorce in accordance with the terms of the agreement. In almost every state, the work product of a mediator, a separation agreement, will expedite a divorce.

Now that fault issues have been eliminated in the divorce laws of many states, divorce courts are more concerned with dividing the marital property, not only things like houses and cars, and bank accounts, and stocks and bonds, but novel forms of property as well—rights to pensions and intangible assets and the income from a career. Determining what is a marital asset and allocating it between the parties has become a major concern in contested divorces.

Divorce lawyers have become familiar with esoteric areas: pension plans, stock options, and group health plans. The cost of purchasing comprehensive health coverage can be prohibitive, several thousand dollars in some cases. That can be a substantial sum for a woman who is going through a divorce. Her lawyer must know how to protect her. At least one state, Massachusetts, has passed a law giving the dependent spouse the right to remain in a company group health plan until the wage earner remarries. This is the kind of information that a divorce lawyer must have and that a mediator should know as well.

What laws apply to unmarried couples who split up?

Even unmarried couples may have mutual obligations. In a well-publicized California case, *Marvin* v. *Marvin* (1976), an unmarried woman, after living with a wealthy actor for seven years, claimed half of the property he had acquired during that period, plus support payments. She said that he had agreed to compensate her. His lawyer argued that her claim was based on an immoral relationship. Initially her claim was dismissed. She took an appeal.

A couple doesn't have to be married to acquire obligations. Courts may base liability upon the woman's reasonable expectations, using theories of implied contract, constructive trust, or *quantum meruit*. These fancy terms simply mean that the man "ought to pay." In *Marvin* the appellate court remanded the case to determine whether there had been a contract. The trial court ordered Marvin to pay $104,000 to rehabilitate his friend's career (*Marvin v. Marvin,* 1980). The case gave rise to the term "palimony": after a divorce, a wife may get alimony; after lovers split up, the gal may get palimony.

At one time, someone who agreed to marry a girl and bailed out could be sued. Most states now exclude that theory of action. However, money paid to a fiancée as an advance against the marriage may still be recovered. In such situations, negotiating may be required to untangle the parties' property. As couples increasingly live together without being married, these disputes are certain to grow in number.

One man asked his first wife to move back into his home three years after their divorce. She agreed to do so if he would divorce his second wife. She also wanted to be paid a salary for the work she would be doing in his firm and to be given an independent bank account and an interest in the firm. After five years of living together on this basis, the two separated for good. Then, the woman filed a lawsuit claiming community property as a wife. The court held her to her deal. As an unmarried cohabitant, she was not covered by the community property law.

As American couples come together, marry, separate, and divorce, a kaleidoscope effect takes place. The parties' shifting rights and responsibilities must be sorted out as each change takes place. Usually the individuals involved, after some wrangling and bargaining, can work out their problems. Sometimes a family mediator can help them. Only the most intractable cases must be determined in court.

What is contained in a separation agreement?

Facts and circumstances vary. Local law may require special provisions. Drafting a final separation agreement is beyond the scope of mediation and should be reserved for the parties' lawyers.

In general, the separation agreement allocates the family property, provides financial support if it is required, and arranges for custody. The document should include whatever other conditions may be helpful to regulate the parties' relationship in the future. Separation agreements usually contain the following terms:

- Agree to live apart.
- Divide the property, real and personal.
- Establish the amount of alimony.
- Describe the terms of custody and child support.
- Allocate educational and medical expenses.
- Fix insurance and taxes.

Legal fees and expenses may be covered in a separate agreement. The mediator's fees can be handled in the same way, either shared equally between the parties or allocated in some other acceptable way.

What is the normal arrangement for custody?

As we have seen, courts used to give custody to the father on the theory that he owned the children. Then the pendulum swung the other way: courts awarded custody to the mother. Now the courts have adopted a somewhat more liberal approach, attempting to focus on the interests of the child. Often state law contains specific standards that the court must consider. These standards are frequently taken from the Uniform Marriage and Divorce Act. The applicable law should be consulted.

A custody contest may involve an agonizing battle between the attorneys, as each submits expert testimony from a battery of psychiatrists, social workers, and psychologists. Each case requires the court to determine the best interests of the child, now and in the future. Many judges continue to favor the mother, particularly if the child is young and the mother has been the primary caretaker.

A mediator may follow a somewhat similar approach. The mediator, like the judge, will bear in mind that the interests of the child are important. But rather than impose a judgment, based upon the opinions of mental health experts, the mediator will encourage the parents to decide what is best for their child.

Some judges would not give parents that freedom. For example, in the 1962 case of *Ford* v. *Ford,* Justice Black of the United States Supreme Court wrote, "Unfortunately, experience has shown the question of custody, so vital to a child's happiness and well-being, frequently cannot be left to the discretion of the parents. This is particularly true where, as here, the estrangement of husband and wife beclouds judgment with emotion and prejudice."

The parents should be encouraged to think of themselves as partners in childrearing, designing an arrangement that best suits everyone's needs. Many parents need help with this task—they are seldom familiar with all of the available options for custody. An experienced mediator can help the parents select an arrangement to fit the needs of their children.

What happens if a noncustodial parent takes a child away?

One important recent trend has been the widespread passage of the Uniform Child Custody Jurisdiction Act. The primary purpose of this law is to reduce the number of controversies over child custody. Forty-eight states have already passed the law. It is intended to deter child abductions and to provide interstate assistance in adjudicating custody cases. Some states have made child snatching a crime. In 1980, Congress enacted the Parental Kidnapping Prevention Act, which requires state courts to enforce custody decrees from other states. Now the FBI is authorized to investigate kidnappings by parents. Mediators and lawyers should be aware of these laws and should warn their clients that they can get into deep trouble if they violate a custody decree.

Can the custodial parent move away with the child?

When a parent with custody wants to move away, the other parent may go to court to block the move. The judge must decide whether the move is being made for legitimate reasons. How will it affect the child? These decisions are difficult to forecast. A New York judge refused to permit a woman to move with her child to Las Vegas to start a career as a singer, but other courts have allowed moves in which the purpose was to obtain a better job or to join a new husband.

These disputes call for mediation. A recent Maryland decision involved a mother who wanted to take her nine year old to South Africa. The father was unable to convince the judge that the move would harm the child. When he expressed concern about political and racial unrest in South Africa, the judge said, "In today's world, if we permitted parents to take their children only to those countries of whose political systems we approve, or where no possible threat of violence could occur, we would probably have to limit travel to the regions of outer space.'' If such a case had been handled through mediation, the parties could have developed much more information about the conditions under which the child would be living. Obviously, that kind of comprehensive discussion is difficult to have in court.

How does a divorce court determine child custody and support?

In recent years, courts have tended to award custody to the mother, ordering the husband to pay whatever support the particular judge decided is reasonable based on the husband's income and the couple's prior standard of living. In short, child support is supposed to reflect need and ability to pay.

It is difficult, however, to determine in advance how much support a judge is likely to order. Divorce lawyers often guess incorrectly: the court may award inadequate support or leave the husband staggering under an impossible burden. The unpredictability of judicial decisions has encouraged many couples to negotiate arrangements on their own.

Changed judicial attitudes toward divorce reflect a new approach to child custody and support. Some judges believe that father and mother should be treated equally and that children should continue to have contact with both parents. As women earn more substantial salaries, they undoubtedly will be expected to pay a larger share of child support. This is a controversial and changing area of the law. The Uniform Child Custody Jurisdiction Act attempted to harmonize the treatment of custody questions. A mediator should be aware of local law on this subject.

Must parents support their children?

Family responsibility acts impose obligations upon husbands and wives to support each other. Before such laws
were passed, a husband had to support his wife. The statutes equalized that duty. Usually, the degree of support
extends only to necessities: state statutes generally require
payment of "appropriate expenses." While the members
of a family are living together, the appropriateness of the
family's standard of living is regarded as a private matter.
Courts are reluctant to get involved.

The level at which a parent supports dependent children
is also a private matter. In some instances, disputes arise.
For example, the parent may refuse to provide support
unless the child submits to reasonable parental regulations.
In one case, a young woman was being supported by her
father while attending college in another state. Her father
discovered that she had moved out of the college dormitory
and was flunking. He asked her to return home. When she
refused, he stopped supporting her. The court sided with
the father and did not require him to provide further support. The daughter had forfeited her right to be supported
by her father.

The parents' legal obligation continues until the children reach majority. Some jurisdictions impose a continuing duty to support a retarded child or one requiring regular
medical care.

A New York court enforced an oral agreement by a
father to pay his daughter's tuition if she attended a college
within commuting distance. However, two of the five
judges disagreed because the offer had not been made in
writing. In a New Hampshire case, parents were required
to pay college expenses for an adult daughter.

When parents refuse to pay such expenses, a mediator
might suggest various ways to resolve the problem. A negotiated agreement would be preferable to litigation.

Sometimes the cases involve such intimate matters that
one wonders why the parties did not resolve them pri-

vately. In one case, a man gave his girlfriend a jar of his sperm so that she could impregnate herself. When the child was born, the father sued to establish his parental rights. He wanted the court to say that he was the natural father so that he could assume the responsibilities and privileges of parenthood. The court held in his favor. In another case, a court held that a man was not obligated to support a child his wife conceived outside their marriage. Under common law, stepparents are under no legal obligation to support the children of their spouses, although they often accept such duties voluntarily. On the other hand, in conventional artificial insemination cases, courts have held that the husband should be legally responsible: the consensual use of a stranger's sperm is tantamount to the husband's acceptance of that sperm as his own. The donor cannot be compelled to support the offspring. It might be better for all concerned if such matters were resolved in a private forum.

Agreements as to child support between stepparents and natural parents often result in controversites. If a stepparent's agreement is not in writing, it may be unenforceable. If the couple separates, the obligation of the stepparent toward the child may terminate. In the case of couples who are not married, the relationship between the steppartner and the child is even less tenable.

Can support be enforced?

The legal remedies for enforcing support are cumbersome. In many situations, court processes don't work. They require expensive legal procedures to force compliance. Often the mother can't afford a lawyer. For collection purposes, the system is archaic. It is not designed for extracting relatively small sums from an absent parent. The father who is supposed to provide support may be difficult to locate. Perhaps he has moved away. Many fathers have concluded that they will never be forced to pay by either the authorities or their former spouse. In many cases, the mother finds it easier to look to the government for support.

In the mid-1970s, Congress attempted to put teeth in the collection process by passing the Child Support and Establishment of Paternity amendments to the Social Security Act. These provisions were intended to make it easier to locate the absent parent. The federal government pays 75 percent of the cost.

Many states have established such programs, but child support is still difficult to collect, particularly after the husband remarries and creates a new family. According to the director of the New Jersey Bureau of Child Support, "A divorced woman today has only a 10 percent chance of being paid on time and in full."

Child support laws have been encouraged by pressure groups of divorced mothers, including the Organization for the Enforcement of Child Support, in Maryland; Parents for the Enforcement of Court Ordered Support, in Connecticut; and FOCUS (For Our Children's Unpaid Support), in Virginia. Working with the Federal Office of Child Support Enforcement or state offices, these groups may help locate a delinquent father.

According to the Federal Office of Child Support Enforcement, over six million women reported delinquent child support payments in 1979. Two or three million more were trying to collect through private channels. State courts have been unable to cope with the volume of such cases.

A few states have passed laws that authorize collection through a wage or pension benefit attachment or by payment into court. As to pension benefits, an additional problem can arise because of the provision in the Employee Retirement Income Security Act that prohibits assignment by anyone other than the worker. The ex-wife may be unable to get her hands on the money.

The weakness in support enforcement programs should be understood by family mediators, particularly those who work with low-income parties. Don't expect too much.

Child support will not necessarily be forthcoming. Here are some points to bear in mind:

- An obligation that falls within the reasonable means of the husband is more likely to be paid.

- If circumstances change so that the obligation becomes onerous, the husband may default.

- An agreement to arbitrate the effect of economic changes may increase the likelihood of payment.

- A buck in the hand is more valuable than a flock of IOUs flying around in the future.

The problem of enforcement should be discussed with the parties before they execute an agreement. The value of the agreement depends upon both parties complying with the obligations they are assuming. Nonsupport is one risk to worry about. There are others. The parent with custody may abandon the child, move to a distant community, or attempt to invalidate the agreement in court. Separation agreements are fragile. They are subject to changing circumstances. Some husbands cut and run. Others suffer serious financial losses. Death, disability, and other disasters pounce upon the best of us. Parties who agree on a formula under the benign influence of a family mediator today may make an unanticipated about-face tomorrow.

All of these considerations argue for attempting to maintain a warm relationship between the children and their father. Cutting off such contact by limiting visitation or by criticizing the father to the children may encourage the delinquency that the wife has most to fear.

If the father is willing to maintain a relationship with his children, there is more chance that he will support them. If mediation reinforces a father's willingness to continue his parenting, it may reduce the likelihood of nonpayment.

Parents without Partners is an organization dedicated to maintaining parental responsibility after a divorce.

There are over twelve million single parents in the United States and Canada. Parents without Partners recognized that the way parents cope with divorce will determine how the children fare. A pamphlet entitled "Parents Are Forever" provides helpful guidelines for divorced parents. According to the pamphlet, visits should be as frequent as possible, with flexible schedules. Usually the parent and the child should be alone together. The visits should include outings and visits to the noncustodial parent's place. Visitation should be fun.

This sounds great, but noncustodial parents often feel rejected, no longer needed by the child. Accordingly, some stop seeing their children. This can lead them to believe that it no longer makes sense to continue child support payments. That would not be in the child's interest, nor would it help the custodial parent.

Will courts award custody to a homosexual parent?

In a recent Virginia decision, a lesbian mother won back her son. The court said that her lifestyle was a factor to be considered but "did not outweigh the clear and convincing evidence that she is a devoted mother and, in every other respect, a fit parent."

Some judges find a homosexual lifestyle "offensive." The question is whether the homosexual is a fit parent. A Massachusetts court said that sexual preference is irrelevant, but a North Dakota court gave the children to their father because the mother was living with another woman in a homosexual relationship. The court explained that homosexuality is not "normal." The Oklahoma Supreme Court also denied custody to a mother who had an open homosexual relationship. The women had been living together with their sons. Even though a psychiatrist testified that a boy raised in such a home was not likely to become a homosexual and recommended that the boy be left with his mother, the court refused custody.

In selecting a mediator, the parties may want to ascertain whether the mediator has an open mind on such subjects.

What if neither parent is fit?

Sometimes neither parent can be given custody. State laws determine how such a finding must be made.

Three children were removed from their parents' home in 1973 after episodes of physical abuse and neglect. In 1978, a New York trial judge terminated the parents' rights on a "preponderance of the evidence" that the children were "permanently neglected." The parents appealed. The New York Court of Appeals dismissed the appeal. The case was then taken to the U.S. Supreme Court. In a five-four decision in 1982, in *Santosky* v. *Kramer,* the Court held that parental rights can be terminated only on a finding of neglect based upon evidence that is "clear and convincing." The case was sent back to New York for another trial.

This case illustrates how difficult it is for our antiquated judicial system to determine the status of children. The Santosky children were placed in foster care in 1973. Nine years later, their case was still pending. A negotiated settlement might have settled the case in 1973 if the parents could have been brought together with representatives of the state.

What are appropriate visitation rights?

For the parent who is not awarded custody, continuing contact with the child is limited to visitation. Sometimes parents will rely on their attorneys to draft that clause in the agreement. Many separation agreements contain visitation provisions giving the father the right to see the child during some limited period. If the parents cannot agree, the court will determine the visitation rights.

When visitation is negotiated by the lawyers, the father's attorney will usually ask for more time with the child. The mother's lawyer may say no visitation at all or offer a strictly limited time with the child. The attorneys may view visitation as a secondary issue, less important than support or custody. In the end, they may compromise. Frequently, every other weekend is selected as an easy midpoint between the clients' initial positions.

A mediator might have the opportunity to create a more suitable formula. The parents should be asked to consider all the alternatives, particularly when both say that they are willing to assume responsibility for the care of their child.

Wallerstein and Kelly (1980) have noticed that children in counseling, after having been involved in a divorce, express "the wish for increased contact with their fathers with a startling and moving intensity." Children who see their fathers only twice a month express "great dissatisfaction." These authors add: "The most pressing demand children brought to counseling was for more visiting. The intense longing for greater contact persisted undiminished over may years, long after divorce was acceptable as an unalterable fact of life" (p. 134).

Visitation is vital to the child's relationship with the absent parent. It seems callous not to listen to a child's preferences, but children are seldom asked their opinion. Later, everyone comes to resent the rigidity of the visitation schedule, particularly when it is strictly policed by one of the parents: "George, you were twenty minutes late today. Last week you came back before you were supposed to. We can't go on this way!"

Sometimes other relatives will want to maintain contact with the child. Forty states have grandparent visitation laws. In a recent Illinois case, the maternal grandparents of a minor child won visitation privileges. The mother was deceased. The child had maintained a close relationship with the grandparents. One wonders why such cases have to be contested in court.

Does a wife always get alimony?

Divorce courts base alimony upon the needs of the person seeking support and the ability of the other party to afford such payments. Some of the other factors that may be considered are the length of the marriage, the age and health of the parties, and their educational level and earning capacity. Recently, courts have emphasized the need to prepare nonworking wives for appropriate employment. Only a few husbands have been awarded alimony; but, as a result of a 1979 U.S. Supreme Court Case, *Orr* v. *Orr*, most states have desexed their alimony laws.

In negotiating a separation agreement, parties should obtain tax advice about whether it is preferable to have support payments described as alimony or family maintenance. Various options are available: lump sum payments, periodic installments in the form of an annuity, or continuing support pending some defined future event.

The agreement should also specify whether the payments to the wife will end if she remarries or constitute part of a property settlement that her remarriage would not terminate.

Finally, the parties must decide whether support payments should be subject to adjustment at some future time. If the husband's income increases, should the wife receive a greater amount? How should such an increase be determined? Some agreements contain an arbitration provision to cope with contingencies.

Arbitration clauses are particularly effective in separation agreements. They encourage good faith bargaining. In the relatively few cases that can't be settled by the parties themselves, an expert arbitrator can be obtained from the American Arbitration Association. The arbitrator can schedule a private hearing and issue a binding award.

Does alimony stop if the wife lives with another man?

Alimony payments terminate when the wife remarries, but when a divorced woman simply moves in with another man, the obligation to pay alimony does not automatically terminate. This may infuriate the woman's former husband. Courts don't express too much sympathy: they point out that the wife never took an oath of chastity and that the new partner has not necessarily agreed to support the woman.

A private detective told me that he often is hired to investigate such cases. When he tells an ex-husband that his former wife is living with another man, the client may stop sending alimony checks: "Sometimes the woman has to take the guy to court. My clients are outraged when the judge tells them that they have to continue paying. They can't believe that they must subsidize some other guy's pleasure. At least, that's how they see it."

A few states have passed laws that terminate alimony if the ex-spouse cohabits with a member of the opposite sex, but sometimes only if it affects the recipient's financial circumstances. As in so many situations, forecasting the results of a domestic relations case requires a close reading of the applicable statute and of the court decisions on the issue.

How long does the agreement stay in effect?

The separation agreement will stay in effect only as long as the parties are living apart. The mediator should warn the parties about this. They may attempt a trial reconciliation, which may void their agreement.

Separation agreements are fragile documents. If the separation agreement "induced" a divorce, it may not be enforceable by either party. This point should be explained to the parties. Family law has its fictions, and this is one of them. Most separation agreements anticipate a divorce.

But if the agreement was based on a promise to divorce, it may be voidable. In short, the agreement has "induced" the divorce. For example, one of the parties may have been persuaded to sign on the basis of a large lump sum payment. When that money is spent, a court may overturn the agreement.

If the couple remarries, claims under the separation agreement are forfeited. The subsequent marriage voids the divorce. The agreement self-destructs.

What is community property?

Arizona, California, Idaho, Louisiana, Nevada, New Mexico, Texas, and Washington have community property laws, under which the parties acquire an undivided interest in property obtained during their marriage. Property acquired either before the marriage or after its dissolution is classified "separate." Property acquired during the marriage is classified "community." Since many forms of property may be involved—earnings, rents, profits, or court awards—the classification process is complicated. For example, gifts and inheritances may be separate even though they were received by one of the individuals during the marriage.

Other questions arise. Who controls the use of community property? Can property be transferred from one category to another by agreement? What restrictions are there on the use of community property?

These issues have significant potential legal and tax implications, and legal questions in community property states can be complex. Divorce terminates the community relationship but unleashes many thorny problems.

Recent court cases have established the principle that a wife who has paid for her husband's professional training during their marriage is entitled, after a divorce, to a share of whatever earnings result from his schooling. As a California judge explained, the student otherwise would "walk away from a marriage with a 'windfall' that might have great value." Similar holdings have been made in Massachusetts, Minnesota, and New Jersey.

What is equitable distribution?

Equitable distribution statutes have been passed in about forty states and are now being defined in court decisions. Novel terminology always presents a challenge to the judiciary. In Pennsylvania, for example, the Court of Common Pleas in Allegheny County said that "equitable" means "equal." The statute in question contains ten factors to be considered in dividing up a divorcing couple's property, including the length of marriage, the age and health of each party, and their sources of income. The court complained that the statute didn't say how much weight to give each factor. Fifty-fifty seemed to be an appropriate starting point.

Equitable distribution laws may increase litigation. They also encourage divorcing parties to negotiate property settlements privately. If a case goes to court, the legal criteria are so complicated that litigation could drag on for years. Just to obtain necessary information could take months of discovery procedures. In states that have adopted equitable distribution, mediation should be particularly attractive. The mediator must be aware of the applicable law because the parties will want to know how a court might split up their property.

Equitable distribution requires that a value be placed on each piece of property to be distributed. How should the parties value their residence? Market value? Appraised value? Fair rental value? And how to calculate their rights in a low-interest-rate mortgage? Is a rent-free home treated as alimony or as nondeductible support? These are quite complicated areas. A mediator who is familiar with property appraisal could be particularly helpful to parties who are attempting to distribute their property on an equitable basis. The bibliography in this book includes many recent articles on equitable distribution, but this area of the law will be swollen with change. A mediator will need to keep in step with developing case law.

What are the tax aspects of divorce?

Tax considerations can be important in settling the financial aspects of separation agreements. The mediator should know something about federal income, estate, and gift taxes and about the various state and local taxes.

The tax implications of alimony, child support, and property transfer can be complicated. Alimony payments are deductible for the person paying the money but are taxable income for the recipient under certain circumstances. It is important that the parties know in advance whether their arrangement will qualify for such treatment. Support generally is paid in accordance with a written agreement, periodically. A lump sum property settlement may not qualify as a tax deduction. The situation can get even muddier when trusts are utilized to cushion the impact of a settlement. Parties are well advised to discuss any unusual formula with a tax advisor before signing their agreement.

The various insurance policies that are in effect or will need to be obtained after the separation or the divorce will also have to be reviewed, particularly regarding their tax impact. The mediator should encourage full disclosure, making sure that the policies are paid up and that both parties know what needs to be done about notifying the insurance companies of their change in status. Often, the wage earner's group life and health coverage will be a vital part of the settlement. The mediator should consult experts if necessary.

For the family mediator, the Internal Revenue Code represents a useful bargaining device in designing an attractive settlement. No property settlement can be discussed intelligently without some consideration of its tax impact. Since the law allows broad discretion in the allocation of the tax burdens associated with a separation, the mediator and the lawyers have a rare opportunity to structure the financial arrangements to the parties' best advantage. Intelligent use of the code can reduce the out-of-pocket costs for the husband or give the wife some tax-free income. Again, a mediator will have to stay up to date with current developments. Tax law changes on almost a month-to-month basis.

Conclusion

As this chapter has demonstrated, family law is a mysterious, always changing, and complicated blueprint for how individuals can operate within a family structure. Each of the fifty state laws is somewhat different although efforts have been made to encourage uniformity. I have encouraged mediators to become familiar with their own local law, not to give legal advice but at least to recognize some of the problems that their clients may face.

Conclusion

INCREASING NUMBERS OF ORGANIZATIONS and individuals are offering mediation services as an alternative to the traditional adversary legal process. This book has attempted to answer many of the questions that potential parties and mediators are asking about this new service. In mediation, parties work together to clarify their problem, identifying areas of agreement and devising ways to achieve a satisfactory arrangement for the future.

Why are families turning to mediation? Simply because many people have concluded that the adversarial system does not help to resolve family disputes. Litigation increases people's hostility and encourages them to seek revenge. It pits one party against another. When a court order is imposed upon one of the parties, it is resented and may be ignored.

In capable hands, mediation can encourage a working relationship, helping to build a sound foundation for the parties' future lives. Many lawyers and mental health professionals are learning how to serve as mediators. This book is intended to inspire them. Beyond that, it is my hope that readers who find themselves in a dispute in their own family will be encouraged to take a positive approach, to ask themselves what a mediator would do.

APPENDIX A

AAA Family Mediation Rules

1. Request for Mediation—Parties may initiate mediation under these Rules by filing a joint request for a family mediator with any Regional Office of the AAA. The request should identify the individuals who are involved in the dispute, with their present addresses and phone numbers, and should briefly describe the controversy and the issues involved. The parties should include whatever information would be helpful to the AAA in appointing a mediator.

2. Appointment of Mediator—Upon receipt of a joint request for mediation, the AAA will recommend a mediator from its local panel. The parties will be given information about the mediator being proposed. In most cases, the mediator will have had no past or present relationship with the parties. A mediator recommended by the AAA is free to refuse the appointment or to resign at any time.

3. Vacancies—If any mediator shall become unwilling or unable to serve or if one of the parties requests the mediator to

resign from the case, the parties may request the AAA to recommend another mediator.

4. Representation by Counsel—Parties normally are not
represented by counsel at the mediation sessions but are encouraged to seek independent legal advice about the process or
as to any legal issues that may arise.

5. Time and Place—The mediator will arrange the time and
place for each conference with the parties. Conferences are
scheduled directly by the mediator.

6. Identification of Matters in Dispute—The mediator may
request the parties to provide in advance a memorandum providing information about themselves, the problems confronting
them, and the issues that need to be resolved.

7. Guidelines for the Parties and the Mediator—A mediator
does not have authority to impose a settlement upon the parties
but will attempt to help the parties reach a satisfactory resolution of their dispute. The mediator does not provide legal advice
or psychological counseling.

8. Full Disclosure of Relevant Information—At the first conference, the parties will be expected to produce all information
reasonably required for the mediator to understand the issues
presented. The mediator may require either party to supplement
such information.

9. Attendance at Conferences—Conferences are private.
The mediator may sometimes meet with both parties, sometimes
with one of them privately. Other persons may attend only with
the permission of the parties, and at the invitation of the mediator.

10. Mediator's Right to Interview Child—The mediator may
want to interview a child privately, to determine the child's
attitude towards custodial arrangements or visitation rights.
Such an interview may be arranged if both parties agree. In
conducting such an interview, the mediator should not encourage the child to choose between the parents.

11. Professional Opinion as to Best Interests of Child—With
the approval of both parties, the mediator may obtain a professional opinion as to the best interests of a child. The opinion
will be shared with the parties. The cost will be shared by
them.

12. Agreements on Issues—In the event of an agreement,
the mediator will record the understanding of the parties. The

mediator's report may be submitted by the parties to their personal attorneys for incorporation in a formal document.

13. Confidentiality—Confidential information disclosed by the parties or by witnesses to a mediator in the course of the mediation shall not be divulged by the mediator. All records, reports, or other documents received by a mediator while serving in such capacity shall be confidential. The mediator shall not be compelled to divulge such records or to testify in regard to the mediation on behalf of either party in an adversary proceeding or judicial forum.

14. Immunity from Liability or Process—Neither the mediator nor the AAA may be held liable for their performance hereunder. The parties agree not to include the mediator or the AAA as a party or witness in any judicial proceedings involving their relationship or the mediation.

15. Interpretation and Application of Rules—The mediator shall interpret and apply these Rules insofar as they relate to the mediator's duties and responsibilities. All other Rules shall be interpreted and applied by the AAA.

Arbitration Rules for the Interpretation of Separation Agreements

1. Initiation of Arbitration—Either party may initiate arbitration under these Rules by filing a Demand for Arbitration with any regional office of the AAA, enclosing a copy of the separation agreement containing an arbitration provision and a brief description of the matter in dispute. Parties to a separation agreement that does not provide for arbitration under the Rules of the AAA may file a joint request for arbitration hereunder.

2. Change of Claim—After filing of the claim, if either party desires to make any new or different claim, such claim shall be made in writing and filed with the AAA, and a copy thereof shall be mailed to the other party, who shall have a period of seven (7) days from the date of such mailing within which to file an answer with the AAA. After the Arbitrator is appointed, however, no new or different claim may be submitted except with the Arbitrator's consent.

3. Appointment of Arbitrator—The AAA shall appoint one or more Arbitrators from its National Panel of Marital Arbitrators. A person appointed as Arbitrator shall disclose to the AAA any circumstances likely to create an impression of bias or any past or present relationship with the parties. Based upon such information, and the comments of the parties, the AAA shall decide whether the Arbitrator should serve and shall inform the parties of its decision, which shall be conclusive.

4. Vacancies—If any Arbitrator should resign, die, be disqualified, or otherwise be unable to serve, the AAA may declare the office vacant. Vacancies shall be filled in accordance with Rule 3.

5. Representation by Counsel—Any party may be represented by counsel.

6. Fixing of Locale—The parties may mutually agree on the locale where the arbitration is to be held. If the locale is not designated within seven (7) days from the date of filing the Demand or Submission, the AAA shall have power to determine the locale. Its decision shall be final and binding. If any party requests that the hearing be held in a specific locale and the other party files no objection thereto within seven (7) days after the request, the locale shall be the one requested.

7. Time and Place—The Arbitrator shall fix the time and place for each hearing. The AAA shall mail to each party notice of the first hearing at least seven (7) days in advance, unless the parties by mutual agreement waive such notice.

8. Full Disclosure of Assets—At the first hearing, if economic issues are involved, the parties shall produce all information reasonably required to provide a full and complete statement of assets and liabilities, including financial statements presently prepared and previously furnished to others, income tax returns, and bank statements. The Arbitrator may require either party to supplement such information as to such assets or as to anticipated economic needs.

9. Attendance at Hearings—Hearings are private. Both parties are entitled to attend, but children and other interested persons may be present only with the permission of the Arbitrator. The Arbitrator may require the retirement of any witness not a party during the testimony of other witnesses.

10. Arbitration in the Absence of a Party—Unless the law provides to the contrary, the arbitration may proceed in the absence of any party who, after due notice, fails to be present or fails to obtain an adjournment. An award shall not be made solely on the default of a party. The Arbitrator shall require the party who is present to submit such evidence as the Arbitrator may require for the making of an award.

11. Evidence—The Arbitrator shall have broad discretion as to how testimony and evidence shall be received. The hearings shall be informal. In addition to direct statements from the parties, the Arbitrator may receive documents and affidavits, giving them such weight as they may merit.

12. Arbitrator's Right to Interview Child—In custody-related issues, the Arbitrator is authorized to interview a child privately in order to ascertain the child's needs as to custodial arrangements and visitation rights. In conducting such an interview, the Arbitrator shall avoid forcing the child to choose between parents or to reject either of them.

13. Professional Opinion as to Best Interests of Child—With the approval of both parties, the Arbitrator may obtain a professional opinion relevant to the best interests of the child. Such an opinion shall be submitted to both parties in sufficient time for them to comment thereon to the Arbitrator before the hearings are closed. The cost thereof shall be shared by the parties.

14. Adjournments—The Arbitrator may take adjournments upon the request of a party or at the Arbitrator's initiative, and shall take such adjournment when all of the parties agree thereto.

15. Temporary Court Order—During arbitration, either party may request a court of competent jurisdiction to issue a temporary injunction:

(a) to restrain any party from transferring, encumbering, concealing, or in any way disposing of property except in the usual course of business or for the necessities of life and to require the party to account to the court for all extraordinary expenditures made after the order is issued

(b) to enjoin a party from molesting or disturbing the peace of the other party or of any child

(c) to exclude a party from the family home or from the home of the other party when there is evidence that physical or emotional harm would otherwise result

(d) to enjoin a party from removing a child from the jurisdiction

(e) for other injunctive relief proper under the circumstances
No such application to a court shall be deemed a waiver of the party's right to arbitrate.

16. Closing of Hearings—The Arbitrator shall specifically inquire of both parties whether they have any further proofs to offer or witnesses to be heard. Upon receiving negative replies, the Arbitrator shall declare the hearings closed and a minute thereof shall be recorded. If further documents are to be filed, the hearings shall be declared closed as of the final date set by the Arbitrator for their receipt.

17. Reopening of Hearings—The hearings may be reopened by the Arbitrator independently or at the request of either party at any time before the award is made.

18. Extension of Time—The parties may modify any period of time by mutual agreement. The AAA for good cause may extend any period of time established by these Rules, except the time for making the award. The AAA shall notify the parties of any such extension of time and its reason therefor.

19. Time of Award—An award shall be made promptly by the Arbitrator and, unless otherwise agreed by the parties or specified by law, no later than thirty (30) days from the date of closing the hearings.

20. Form and Scope of Award—The award of the Arbitrator shall be in writing and shall be signed either by the sole Arbitrator or by at least a majority if there be more than one. It shall be executed in the manner required by law. The Arbitrator may assess arbitration fees and expenses in favor of either or both parties.

21. Delivery of Award to Parties—Parties shall accept as legal delivery of the award the placing of the award or a true copy thereof in the mail by the AAA, addressed to such party at its last known address or to its attorney, or personal service of the award, or the filing of the award in any manner which may be prescribed by law.

22. Applications to Court—The parties agree not to include the Arbitrator or the AAA as a party or as a witness in any judicial proceedings relating to the arbitration or to any subsequent petition to a court for enforcement of the award or of the separation agreement itself.

23. Interpretation and Application of Rules—The Arbitrator shall interpret and apply these Rules insofar as they relate to the Arbitrator's powers and duties. When there is more than one Arbitrator and a difference arises among them concerning the meaning or application of any such Rule, it shall be decided by a majority vote. If that is unobtainable, either an Arbitrator or a party may refer the question to the AAA for final decision. All other Rules shall be interpreted and applied by the AAA.

Model Three-Day Family Mediation Training Program (Sponsored by the AAA)

DAY ONE

9:00 *PROGRAM INTRODUCTION*

9:15 *INTRODUCTION TO FAMILY MEDIATION*

- An overview of family mediation, explaining what it is and describing the evolution of this alternative as a response to the needs of families.

- Comparison of mediation with traditional divorce litigation process.

- A survey of the various ways that mediation is now being practiced under court and private auspices.

Faculty: Family mediator

10:30 *PROCESS OF MEDIATION*

- A presentation describing the mediation process, focusing on the goals of mediation, how it is done, and the role of a mediator as a neutral.

- Focus on the central element of negotiation.

    Faculty: Panel or experienced family mediator

12:00 *LUNCH/FILM:* "Conflict on Travis Avenue," a training film produced by the AAA

- A discussion of the film.

1:00 *ANALYSIS OF MEDIATION PROCESS*

- An experienced family mediator will role-play a mediation session with a couple. Trainer will use a technique in which the role playing is interrupted in order to provide an opportunity for the participants to discuss the mediator's strategy. The participants observe the action and write down their personal comments and questions.

    Faculty: Family mediator and staff support

3:15 *LEGAL FRAMEWORK OF DIVORCE MEDIATION*

- An expert will brief the participants on the legal aspects of separation and divorce, including matrimonial law, grounds for divorce, division of property, and spousal and child support.

- The legal status of the mediation process.

- Difference between mediation and practicing law: ethical problems.

    Faculty: Matrimonial attorney experienced in mediation.

DAY TWO

9:00– *EMOTIONAL DYNAMICS OF DIVORCE*
10:00
- Analysis of some of the common dynamics of divorcing couples and how they may affect the mediation process.

- Possible indicators of these dynamics and strategies for the mediator.

    Faculty: Panel—counselor, social worker, and mediator

10:00– *MEDIATION SIMULATIONS AND CRITIQUE* (Sand-
4:00   wich lunch served at noon.)

- Participants will role-play two different scenarios of separating couples in mediation; different participants will role-play the mediator in the two exercises.

- Experienced mediators will observe the exercises and offer critique and spark discussion concerning technique and strategy.

    Faculty: Family mediators

DAY THREE

9:00 *PLANNING CUSTODY SETTLEMENTS*

- A presentation on the rationale and structure of various custody arrangements, with consideration of family structure and needs of the children and parents.

    Faculty: Panel—mediator, family counselor, and social worker

11:00 *PLANNING SPOUSAL SUPPORT AND PROPERTY SETTLEMENTS*

- A focus on the variations in spousal support arrangements and creative property settlements.

    Faculty: Matrimonial attorney

12:30 *LUNCH/PRESENTATION: "Setting up a Family Mediation Practice"*

- A discussion of key issues related to setting up a mediation practice, realistic caseload, insurance, linking with professional organizations and with AAA.

Faculty: Practicing family mediator

2:00 *ECONOMIC DIMENSIONS OF DIVORCE*

- A presentation on the economic realities and issues of separation and divorce, incluidng:
- financial planning
- financial investigation
- tax considerations
- future life planning

Faculty: Matrimonial attorney and financial planner

4:00 *CONCLUSION*

APPENDIX D

AAA Sample Form Retainer Agreement

_____ and _____ (the parties) have jointly requested _____ to act as their mediator in accordance with the Family Mediation Rules of the American Arbitration Association. The controversy between the parties concerns the terms of a separation agreement. The parties agree to negotiate in good faith toward such a settlement and to provide the mediator with full and accurate information about the case.

The mediator has accepted the parties' request and will provide mediation services to them on an impartial basis. The time and place of mediation will be set at the convenience of the parties and will be held in accordance with the above Rules.

The mediator has advised the parties that conflicts are likely to arise between them during the course of negotiations. To protect their legal rights, each party is encouraged to seek advice from counsel. There is no limitation on the right to seek such advice at any time during the mediation. Each party should advise the mediator of the name and telephone number of counsel.

The mediator has also advised the parties that they may terminate the mediation at any point, paying the mediator only what has accrued to that time. The mediator in turn reserves the right to resign from the case at any time.

The mediator acknowledges that all information received by the mediator during this procedure will be confidential. The mediator will not divulge such information to any third person without the consent of both parties. The mediator urges the parties, on their part, to keep such information confidential so that there can be a full and candid exchange.

The parties agree not to hold either the mediator or the AAA liable or to include either in any judicial proceedings involving the mediation or the parties' relationship. The mediator agrees not to represent or give support to either party in any subsequent matter or proceeding. The mediator will not provide any legal opinion as to the law or any other aspect of the case.

It is up to the parties themselves to negotiate their own agreement. If the parties are able to reach an agreement, the mediator will prepare a memorandum recording that understanding which may then be submitted to the parties' personal attorneys for incorporation into a formal separation agreement.

Each party agrees, during the course of the mediation, to respect the privacy of the other and not to transfer disputed property or assume additional debts without mutual consent. All interim agreements will be discussed with the mediator before being entered into.

The mediator's fees are $____ an hour, plus any costs incurred. Both parties will be billed monthly for the entire outstanding amount for which they will be jointly liable.

_____   _____

Mediator   Party

____   _____

Date   Party

References

Introduction

NAGLER, MICHAEL N. 1982. *America Without Violence.* Covelo, Calif.: Island Press, p. 96.

Chapter 1. Mediating Family Disputes

American Family. 1981. Vol. IV, no. 4.

COOGLER, O. J. 1979. *Structured Mediation in Divorce Settlements.* Lexington, Mass.: Heath.

PEARSON, JESSICA. 1982. "Mediation and Divorce: The Benefits Outweigh the Costs." *Colorado Lawyer,* February.

PERRY, M. J. 1980. *California Living, the Magazine of the San Francisco Sunday Examiner and Chronicle,* October 26.

RISKIN, LEONARD L. 1982. *Ohio State Law Journal 43,* 1, pp. 29–60.

Chapter 2. Family Mediation in Action

COOGLER, O. J. 1979. *Structured Mediation in Divorce Settlements.* Lexington, Mass.: Heath.
HAYNES, JOHN M. 1981. *Divorce Mediation: A Practical Guide for Therapists and Counselors.* New York: Springer.

Chapter 3. Divorce Mediation: A New Profession

MILNE, ANN L. 1978. "Custody of Children in a Divorce Process: A Family Self-Determination Model." *Conciliaton Courts Review 16,* pp. 2–12.
RICCI, ISOLINA. 1980. *Mom's House/Dad's House: Making Shared Custody Work.* New York: Macmillan.
WALLERSTEIN, JUDITH S., and JOAN BERLIN KELLY. 1980. *Surviving the Breakup.* New York: Basic Books.

Chapter 4. How to Act as a Family Mediator

Association of the Bar of the City of New York. 1981. *Committee on Professional and Judicial Ethics,* no. 80-23, February 27.
Kenworthy v. *Kenworthy.* 1980. 180 Conn. 129.
Lange v. *Marshall.* 1981. *Family Law Reporter 7,* p. 2583 (Mo. Ct. App.).
Levine v. *Levine.* 1981. *Family Law Reporter 7,* p. 2613 (App. Div., 2d Dep.).
SILBERMAN, LINDA J. 1981. "Professional Responsibility: Problems of Divorce Mediation." *Family Law Reporter 7,* 15, pp. 4001–4012.

Chapter 5. Family Disputes and the Law

FREED, DORIS J., and HENRY H. FOSTER. 1982. "Family Law in the Fifty States." *Family Law Reporter 8,* pp. 4065–4104.
KATZ, SANFORD N. 1981. "Equitable Distribution Continues to Make Gains" (ABA Section of Family Law 1980–1981 Developments). *National Law Journal 3* (August 10), p. 43.
Marvin v. *Marvin.* 1976. 557 P.2d 106 (Calif.).
Marvin v. *Marvin.* 1980. 5 FLR 3077 Calif. Superior Ct. 4118179.

Orr v. *Orr*. 1979. 440 U.S. 268.

Santosky v. *Kramer*. 1982. 102 S.Ct. 1388 (U.S. Supreme Court).

WALLERSTEIN, JUDITH S., and JOAN BERLIN KELLY. 1980. *Surviving the Breakup*. New York: Basic Books.

Selected Bibliography on Family Mediation and Related Topics*

Mediation

BAHR, STEVEN J. 1980. *Divorce Mediation: An Evaluation of an Alternative Divorce Policy*. Chapel Hill: Bush Institute for Child and Family Policy, University of North Carolina.

———. 1981. "Mediation Is the Answer." *Family Advocate 3*, pp. 32–35.

COOGLER, O. J. 1977. "Changing the Lawyer's Role in Matrimonial Practice." *Conciliation Courts Review 15*, p. 1.

———. 1978. *Structured Mediation in Divorce Settlement: A Handbook for Marital Mediators*. Lexington, Mass.: Heath.

———, RUTH E. WEBER, and PATRICK C. McKENRY. 1979. "Divorce Mediation: A Means of Facilitating Divorce Adjustment." *Family Coordinator 28*, p. 255.

CROUCH, RICHARD E. 1982. "Mediation and Divorce: The Dark Side Is Still Unexplored." *Family Advocate 4*, pp. 27, 33–35.

* Compiled by the Eastman Arbitration Library of the American Arbitration Association, Laura F. Brown, Librarian, New York, N.Y.

DISHON, MICHAEL. 1981a. "Family Divorce Mediation: Attorneys, Are You Ready?" *Los Angeles Daily Journal 94* (April 7), p. 4.

———. 1981b. "Marital Conflict and Resolution." *Los Angeles Daily Journal 94* (June 16), p. 4.

———. 1981c. "The Divorce Mediator's Role and the Stage of Mediation." *Los Angeles Daily Journal 94* (June 30), p. 4.

"Divorce California Style: Benefits of Mediation." *New Jersey Law Journal 107* (January 29), p. 15.

EARLY, MAUREEN. 1981. "Divorce Mediation: Both Sides Can Feel They Won." *Newsday,* March 17.

EGLASH, ALBERT. 1981a. *Meditating and Negotiating Your Divorce: A Handbook for Divorcing Couples.* San Luis Obispo: Quest.

———. 1981b. *Mediation, the Conciliatory Spirit: A Collection of Essays for Divorce Mediators.* San Luis Obispo: Quest.

FAMILY MEDIATION ASSOCIATION. 1976. *Marital Mediation Divorce Settlement with Less Stress.* Atlanta: Family Mediation Association.

FISKE, JOHN A. 1979. "Divorce Mediation as a Less Painful Path." *Massachusetts Lawyers Weekly 8,* 1, p. 7.

FULLER, LON L. 1971. "Mediation: Its Forms and Functions." *Southern California Law Review 44,* 2, pp. 305–339.

GALANTE, MARY ANN. 1981. "Private Mediation: The Lawyer as a Peacemaker." *Los Angeles Lawyer 4* (December), p. 18.

———. 1982. "The One-Lawyer Divorce." *National Law Journal 4* (January 25), p. 1.

GAUGHAN, LAWRENCE D. 1981. "Taking a Fresh Look at Divorce Mediation." *Trial 17,* 4, pp. 39–41.

GOLD, LOIS. 1981. "Mediation in the Dissolution of Marriage." *Arbitration Journal 36,* 3, pp. 9–13.

HARBINSON, KIMBERLY TALOR. 1981. "Family Law: Attorney Mediation of Marital Disputes and Conflict of Interest Considerations." *North Carolina Law Review 60* (October), pp. 171–184.

HARRIS, M. 1980. "Divorce's Friendly Persuaders [Mediators]." *Money 9* (April), p. 85.

HAYNES, JOHN M. 1978. "Divorce Mediator: A New Role." *Social Work 23* (January), pp. 5–9.

———. 1981. *Divorce Mediation: A Practical Guide for Therapists and Counselors.* New York: Springer.

HERRMAN, MARGARET S., PATRICK C. McKENRY, and RUTH E. WEBER. 1979. "Mediation and Arbitration Applied to Family Conflict Resolution." *Arbitration Journal 34,* 1, pp. 17–21.

HEYMANN, L. 1981. "Mediation Helps Couples [Divorce Mediation]." *Humanist 41* (September/October), p. 21.

IRVING, HOWARD H. 1980. *Divorce Mediation: A Rational Alternative to the Adversary System*. New York: Universe.

JENKINS, JOHN A. 1981a. "Divorce California Style." *Student Lawyer 9* (January), p. 30.

——. 1981b. "Split Decisions: Mediation Is Helping Divorcing Couples Get It Together." *TWA Ambassador* (March), p. 28.

KLEMESRUD, JUDY. 1981. "Mediating a Less Hostile End to a Marriage." *New York Times*, August 3, p. B5.

MERONEY, ANNE E. 1979. "Mediation and Arbitration of Separation and Divorce Agreements." *Wake Forest Law Review 15*, 4, pp. 467–486.

MILNE, ANN L. 1978. "Custody of Children in a Divorce Process." *Conciliation Courts Review 16*, pp. 2–12.

MNOOKIN, ROBERT, and LEWIS KORNHAUSER. 1979. "Private Bargaining in the Shadow of the Law." *Yale Law Journal 88*, p. 950.

MOSKOWITZ, LAWRENCE A. 1978. "Divorce-Custody Dispositions: The Child's Wishes in Perspective." *Santa Clara Law Review 18*, 2, pp. 427–452.

"Non-judicial Resolution of Custody and Visitation Disputes." 1979. *University of California, Davis, Law Review 12*, 1, pp. 582–603.

PEARSON, JESSICA. 1981a. "Child Custody: Why Not Let the Parents Decide?" *Judges' Journal 20*, 1, p. 4.

——. 1981b. "How Child Custody Mediation Works in Practice." *Judges' Journal 20*, 1, pp. 11–12.

——, and LOIS VANDER KOOI. 1980. "Mediation Project." *Colorado Lawyer 9* (April), p. 712.

——, and NANCY THEONNES. 1982. "Mediation and Divorce: The Benefits Outweigh the Cost." *Family Advocate 4*, 3, pp. 26, 28–32.

PICKRELL, ROBERT W., and ALICE L. BENDHEIM. 1980. "Family Disputes Mediation: A New Service for Lawyers and Their Clients." *Barrister 7*, 1, pp. 27–28.

SALIUS, A. 1978. "The Use of Mediation in Contested Custody and Visitation Cases in the Family Relations Court." Manuscript, Hartford, Connecticut, Superior Court.

SILBERMAN, LINDA J. 1981. "Professional Responsibility: Problems of Divorce Mediation." *Family Law Reporter 7*, 15, pp. 4001–4012.

SPENCER, JANET, and JOSEPH P. ZAMMIT, 1976. "Mediation-Arbitration: A Proposal for Private Resolution of Disputes between Divorced or Separated Parents." *Duke Law Journal 1976*, 5, pp. 911–939.

STEWART, HELEN M. 1976. *Domestic Mediation Project: Initial Development Report*. Boston: American Arbitration Association.

STULBERG, MIDGE COWAP. 1980. "When Three Is Not a Crowd." *Family Advocate 12*, 4, pp. 4–5.

VROOM, PATRICIA, DIANE FASSETT, and ROWAN A. WAKEFIELD. 1981. "Mediation: The Wave of the Future?" *American Family 4*, 4, pp. 8–13.

———. 1982. "Winning Through Mediation: Divorce Without Losers." *Futurist* (February), pp. 28–34.

WALLERSTEIN, J. S., and J. KELLY. 1980. *Surviving the Breakup*. New York: Basic Books.

WINKS, PATRICIA L. 1981. "Divorce Mediation: A Nonadversary Procedure for the No-fault Divorce." *Journal of Family Law 19* (August), pp. 615–653.

WISEMAN, J. M., and JOHN A. FISKE. 1980. "Lawyer-Therapist Team as Mediator in a Marital Crisis." *Social Work 25* (November), pp. 442–445.

Conciliation

BARTEAU, BETTY. 1980. "How to Create a Conciliation Court." *Family Advocate 2*, 4, pp. 6–7, 34–35.

FOSTER, HENRY H., JR. 1966. "Conciliation and Counseling in the Courts in Family Law Cases." *New York University Law Review 41*, 2, pp. 353–381.

HOLMAN, NANCY ANN. 1973. "A Law in the Spirit of Conciliation and Understanding: Washington's Marriage Dissolution Act." *Gonzaga Law Review 9* (Fall), pp. 39–56.

IRVING, HOWARD, and BARBARA IRVING. 1975. "Conciliation in Divorce Litigation." *Reports of Family Law 16* (March), pp. 712–724.

LIGHTMAN, ERNIE S., and HOWARD M. IRVING. 1976. *Conciliation and Arbitration in Family Disputes*. Toronto: School of Social Work, University of Toronto, 1976. Also in *Conciliation Courts Review 14*, 2, pp. 12–21.

MADDI, DOROTHY LINDER. 1974. *The Effect of Conciliation Court Proceedings on Petitions for Dissolution of Marriage*. Research Contributions of the American Bar Foundation, no. 6. Chicago:

American Bar Foundation. Also in *Journal of Family Law 13*, pp. 495–566.

ORLANDO, FRANK A. 1978. "Conciliation Programs: Their Effect on Marriage and Family Life." *Florida Bar Journal 52*, 3, pp. 218–221.

SCALETTA, DEAN I. 1981. "Divorce Courts and Conciliation Services: An Interface of Law and the Social Sciences." *Manitoba Law Journal 11* (Summer), pp. 321–328.

TAYLOR, L., and E. WERNER. 1978. "Child Custody and the Conciliation Courts." *Conciliation Courts Review 16*, pp. 25–32.

Arbitration

"Arbitration and Protection of the Child: A Conversation on Implications of *Sheets* v. *Sheets*." 1966. *Arbitration Journal 21*, 4, pp. 215–228.

"Arbitration: A Viable Alternative? Comments." 1974. *Fordham Urban Law Journal 3*, 1, pp. 53–77.

"Arbitration Saved Our Marriage." 1978. *Good Housekeeping*, February, p. 84.

"Arbitration under Separation Agreements." 1961. *Lawyers' Arbitration Letter*, no. 8 (November 15) pp. 1–2.

COULSON, ROBERT. 1969. "Family Arbitration: An Exercise in Sensitivity." *Family Law Quarterly 3* (March), pp. 22–30.

"Domestic Relations Disputes." 1976. *Lawyers' Arbitration Letter*, no. 14 (June), pp. 1–5.

"The Enforceability of Arbitration Clauses in North Carolina Separation Agreements: Comment." 1979. *Wake Forest Law Review 15*, 4, pp. 487–505.

HOLMAN, NANCY ANN, and JANE NOLAND. 1976. "Agreement and Arbitration: Relief to Overlitigation in Domestic Relations Disputes in Washington." *Willamette Law Journal 12*, 3, pp. 527–544.

PAULEY, RAYMOND J. 1975. "Mandatory Arbitration of Support Matters in the Family Courts." *New York State Bar Journal 47* (January), p. 27.

"Validity and Construction of Provision for Arbitration of Disputes to Alimony or Support Payments or Child Visitation or Custody Matters." *American Law Reports* (3d) *18*, p. 1264.

Marriage, Divorce, and the Family

BEAVERS, W. ROBERT. 1977. *Psychotherapy and Growth: A Family Systems Perspective*. New York: Brunner/Mazel.

BORNEMAN, ERNEST, ed. 1976. *The Psychoanalysis of Money*. New York: Urizen.

BRENNER, CHARLES. 1974. *An Elementary Textbook of Psychoanalysis*. Rev. ed. New York: Anchor.

FREED, DORIS J., and HENRY H. FOSTER. 1982. "Family Law in the Fifty States." *Family Law Reporter 8*, pp. 4065–4104.

FREEMAN, D. S. 1980. "The Family as a System: Fact or Fantasy." In John G. Howells, ed., *Advances in Family Psychiatry*, vol. I. New York: International Universities Press.

GARDNER, RICHARD A. 1971. *The Boys' and Girls' Book about Divorce*. New York: Bantam.

———. 1979. *The Parents' Book about Divorce*. New York: Bantam.

GLICK, IRA D., and DAVID R. KESSLER. 1980. *Marital and Family Therapy: An Introductory Text*. New York: Grune & Stratton.

GOLDSTEIN, JOSEPH, ANNA FREUD, and ALBERT SOLNIT. 1973. *Beyond the Best Interests of the Child*. New York: Free Press.

KESSLER, SHEILA. 1975. *The American Way of Divorce: Prescriptions for Change*. Chicago: Nelson-Hall.

PAOLINO, THOMAS J., and BARBARA S. McCRADY. 1980. *Marriage and Marital Therapy*. New York: Brunner/Mazel.

RICCI, ISOLINA. 1980. *Mom's House/Dad's House: Making Shared Custody Work*. New York: Macmillan.

RICHARDS, ARLENE, and IRENE WILLIS. 1977. *How to Get It Together When Your Parents Are Coming Apart*. New York: Bantam.

TRIERE, LYNETTE, and RICHARD PEACOCK. 1982. *Learning to Leave*. Chicago: Contemporary Books.

WALLERSTEIN, JOAN S., and J. KELLY. 1975. *Surviving the Breakup*. New York: Basic Books.

WEISS, ROBERT S. 1975. *Marital Separation*. New York: Basic Books.

WEITZMAN, LENORE J. 1981. "The Economics of Divorce." *UCLA Law Review 28*, 6, p. 1181.

WOOLEY, PERSIA. 1979. *The Custody Handbook*. New York: Summit Books.

Financial Matters

ASPAKLARIA, SHELLEY, and GERSON GELTNER. 1981. *What You Should Know about Your Husband's Money . . . before the Divorce*. New York: Wideview.

AUERBACH, SYLVIA. 1976. *A Woman's Book of Money: A Guide to Financial Independence.* New York: Doubleday.

LEVITAN, SAR, and RICHARD BELOUS. 1981. *What's Happening to the American Family?* Baltimore: Johns Hopkins University Press.

NELSON, PAULA. 1977. *Joy of Money.* New York: Bantam.

ROGERS, MARY. 1981. *Women, Divorce, and Money: Plain Talk about Money, Procedures, Settlements, Financial Survival for Women Who Are Divorced or Thinking about Divorce.* New York: Mc-Graw-Hill.

Equitable Distribution

BRYNTESON, JESSICA C. 1981. "Equitable Distribution in New York." *Albany Law Review 45* (Winter), pp. 483–507.

DIAMOND, BRIAN, and WILLIAM A. PRINSELL. 1980. "New York's Equitable Distribution Law: A Sweeping Reform." *Brooklyn Law Review 47* (Fall), pp. 67–124.

DULLEA, G. 1980. " 'Equitable Distribution' Divorce: Redefining Who Gets What." *New York Times,* June 10, p. B1.

FOSTER, HENRY H., JR. 1981a. "Commentary on Equitable Distribution (New York)." *New York Law School Law Review 26* (Winter), pp. 1–98.

———, ed. 1981b. *A Practical Guide to the New York Equitable Distribution Divorce Law.* New York: Law and Business.

———, and DORIS JONAS FREED. 1981. "Divorce Reform: Equitable v. Equal Distribution of Property." *New York Law Journal 185* (May 28), p. 1.

FOX, M. 1981. "Retroactivity of DRL Barred in Marital Property Actions: Appellate Ruling in Equitable-Distribution Cases." *New York Law Journal 185* (May), p. 1.

FREED, DORIS JONAS, and HENRY H. FOSTER, JR. 1981. "Divorce in the Fifty States." *Family Law Quarterly 14* (Winter), pp. 229–284.

KATZ, SANFORD N. 1981. "Equitable Distribution Continues to Make Gains (ABA Section of Family Law 1980–1981 Developments)." *National Law Journal 3* (August 10), p. 43.

LOOKMAN, JOHN S. 1981. "Equitable Distribution: Some Recommendations." *New York Law Journal 185* (April 10), p. 2.

Matrimonial Practice under Equitable Distribution. 1980. New York: Practicing Law Institute.

MIDDLETON, M. 1980. "New York 'Catches Up': Revises Divorce Law." *American Bar Association Journal 66* (August), p. 950.

TAFT, R. S. 1980. "Equitable Distribution and Tax Planning." *New York Law Journal 184* (October 23), p. 1.

WALLMAN, L. 1980. "Report of the Committee on Legislation, Family Law Section, New York State Bar Association." *New York State Bar Journal 52* (October), pp. 483–485.

Index